# VIOLENCE IN NEW ZEALAND

# IN NEW ZEALAND

## Jane Ritchie &
## James Ritchie

HUIA PUBLISHERS
DAPHNE BRASELL ASSOCIATES PRESS

Second edition co-published in 1993 by
Daphne Brasell Associates Press,
306 Tinakori Road, P.O. Box 12-214, Thorndon, Wellington and
Huia Publishers, 291 Tinakori Road, Thorndon, Wellington,
P.O. Box 17-335, Karori, Wellington, New Zealand

First published in 1990 by Allen and Unwin New Zealand Limited
in association with Port Nicholson Press

National Library of New Zealand
Cataloguing-in-Publication data

Ritchie, Jane, 1936–
    Violence in New Zealand / Jane and James Ritchie. 2nd ed., 1993 ed.
Wellington [N.Z.] : Huia Publishers : Daphne Brasell Associates Press, 1993.
    1 v.
    Includes bibliographical references and index.
    ISBN 0-908975-02-3 (pbk.)
    1. Violence--New Zealand. I. Ritchie, James E. (James Earnest),
1929– II. Title.
    303.60993            zbn93-013784

Cover designed by Sarah Maxey, Daphne Brasell Associates Press
Text offset from the first edition; with the addition of an epilogue and
a preface to the second edition.
Printed and typeset by SRM Production Services, Malaysia

# Contents

# Preface

Most people see violence as a breakdown of social patterns. In this book we present a radical alternative hypothesis, namely, that violence is part of what we are, an expression of deep and extensive cultural patterns. As a society we fail to deal adequately with the violence amongst us because we cling to the first hypothesis and resist accepting the other.

At the level of cultural ideals we want to believe that we are all law abiding and peaceable. But at the level of ideology we have inherited culture patterns that include the coercive use of power, resort to arms, and a leering fascination with sex, aggression and violence. These stimuli are all around us.

When individuals are faced with conflict between aspects of their value system they often disassociate the two elements which are in conflict, acting now on one, then on the other. They deny connections and linkages, especially when, in the cold light of day or logic, they are caught in inconsistency or downright hypocrisy. They distance themselves from the problem, deny its reality, blame others or deny involvement or responsibility. Consequently, nothing changes.

We first began to look at the pattern of violence in New Zealand back in 1963 when we studied the general pattern of child-rearing here. Parents who otherwise did not hit one another (or at least not publicly) not only hit their children but believed that it was good, necessary, right to do so. As we followed this through, we focused on how this pattern persisted over time. We then began to campaign for change in public attitudes towards the punishment of children.

As we researched the matter we found that we had stumbled across a general endorsement of sanctioned violence which we called the ideology of punishment. But it was wider and more extensive in scope and damage than this label implied.

So we moved to the next level of analysis to look at the linkages between all the forms of violent expression in our society. This book is the result.

While we must all do what we can about single events, forms of violence, or violators, while we may focus on any one of a multitude of reasons or causes, we will not achieve much change until we understand the pattern of violence in our culture and society. Is that enough? Maybe not. But we cannot go on tolerating the intolerable, excusing the inexcusable, supporting what we also condemn, pushing responsibility on to others or externals and refusing to make changes to ourselves.

The pattern hinges on the persistence of male role-derived notions of power and privilege to engage in violent acts, and on domestic, public, and individual permissions. It is seen in sporting activity, the glorification of war, on our television screens, on our highways and in other arenas. Women bully sometimes too, throw things, inflict abuse, but the pattern is male. Men must change.

In the many useful published reports on violent offending in New Zealand which must form quite a bookshelf in the office of the Minister of Justice there are hundreds of ideas, recommendations and conclusions, some research based, some not. We have sought to put these into an accessible form. They separately constitute the ingredients of a programme for change but they need comprehensive co-ordination and implementation.

We are not optimistic about outcomes. If you want to fix something, you need to know not only what went wrong but also how to put it right. And you must have the means to do so. There will never be the means until we all put priority on the provision of them, whether they be human, monetary or other resources. Awareness of the pattern is the first step. A real desire to seek change is the next. There is a way ahead; we can all become less violent; we can all call for social change.

This has not been an easy book to write. We have been greatly assisted over the last ten years by our honours students who have read successive drafts. We appreciate their criticism and help.

Jane and James Ritchie
Te Whaanga, April 1990

# Preface to the Second Edition

It is five years since we wrote this book, though the preparation for it began a decade before, and its roots reach back into our first major research study of New Zealand child rearing practices and their consequences, dating from the early 1960s (192).

Violence, far from diminishing over this five year period, has probably increased, and public awareness of it has certainly expanded.

What we are now seeing is a complex mixture of both good news and bad news. The good is demonstrated by a greater willingness to observe, report and act upon violent behaviour which previously was closeted. Provision has been made to deal with the occurrence of child abuse, sexual abuse, partner abuse, rape, uncontrolled anger and its consequences and violence on the roads. But it is too early to assess the effectiveness of these measures.

The bad news is that this awareness itself is not only frightening to many, who might otherwise have lived secure lives in ignorance, but also frightens politicians. The public expects them to do something about it. They have real problems with this because, as this book shows, you cannot effectively deal with violence by merely tinkering with penalties, bail provisions, or details of parole.

Such a focus on violent crime is narrow and short sighted. It does not confront the causes that lie behind the criminal act. We demonstrate in this book that violence is endemic in our society and may, at this point in time, be epidemic.

Those who focus only on crime are not addressing the foundations of violence and, therefore, can only deal, either preventively or punitively, or, less often rehabilitatively, with discrete events.

Similarly, many who take the correction of personal misbehaviour as their target, worthy as their therapeutic efforts may be, cannot address, control or change the contexts within which the offending behaviour occurs.

When, in the preface to the first edition, we located our argument at the level of cultural discourse, some felt that the enormity of the task of culture change presented an impossible goal and an unrealistic programme for change, and that left our readers depressed and hopeless. In the epilogue we will show that there is something everyone can do.

In any case, the last five years show that, in this country, rapid social change is possible. New Zealand is sufficiently small, homogenous, educated and progressive to make changes very quickly. For better or worse, changes to the economy demonstrate this. In addition, and perhaps in reaction to, the negative effects of these changes, there is a current upwelling of social concern about unemployment, poverty and the redefinition of productive effort. Politically, and quite openly, New Zealand has been placed in a state of stress, if not crisis. The outbreak of violence is frequently a consequence of the strain such changes place upon families and individuals. In such a situation many agencies for change, and individual people become activated.

We have not revised the body of the text in this book because, as a review, it stands. We have, however, carried it one step further in an epilogue which will address the practical concern of how this country might construct and coordinate a systematic programme towards the social and cultural goal of becoming less violent.

We briefly report on the last five years. We take the next step beyond the previous final chapter to state explicitly how a programme for the reduction of violence could be constructed and then implemented. Finally, we discuss directly the costs of change, financial and cultural. What, as people, are we prepared to give up in order to live in a less violent society?

*What is Violence?*

# 1

# Introduction

*A woman with small children is half way across a busy intersection when the older child pulls back toward the curb they have just left. Without hesitation the mother pushes the younger child toward the curb ahead and delivers two heavy open-handed blows to the backside of the other who cries loudly while she drags him by the shoulder to the other side of the road.*

*A game of rugby football is in progress. To stop a forward rush in which the forwards are 'hunting' a dropped ball, the open-side flanker has 'gone down' on the ball in order to 'kill it'. The play is close to the flanker's try line and the opposition want quick ball to spin wide. The flanker is overrun by the attacking forwards who, gathered round in what is termed a ruck, drive the opposition forwards off the ball while attempting with their sprigged boots to wrest the ball from the flanker's grasp. He receives a concussion, two broken ribs, multiple bruising, and lacerations.*

*A three-year-old child, living alone with her grandfather, is brought to the hospital because of old scar tissue and recent burns over the entire surface of one hand. Grandfather held the hand of the screaming child over a gas flame to punish her for disobedience.*

*When she became pregnant with her fifth, her husband walked out, blaming and leaving her. The psychiatrist to whom she was referred when she wanted an abortion refused her plea. By then her pregnancy was too far gone to pursue that alternative further. Her husband returned and demanded sexual access, she refused; he beat her, raped her, and broke two of her ribs. Though she escaped to a women's refuge, two years later he was still harassing her.*

*Confronted with an embarrassing question, repeated and pushed home by a resourceful TV interviewer, a senior politician refuses to answer the question, verbally attacks the frontman, and tells the network that he will not be interviewed by that reporter again. The network relegates the interviewer to the children's programmes.*

*A Polynesian ethnic protest group, having repeatedly asked that a group of students desist from imitating Maori posture dances in crude and obscene lampoon style during graduation festivities, finally attacks the offending students with fists, chains, and lengths of timber. Three students require hospital attention.*

*It is 9.45 pm and in the big room at the tavern, proudly publicised as covering half an acre, more than four hundred men and a few women are gathered in varying degrees of intoxication. Shortly, the bar will close and all will be disgorged into the crowded carpark, many clutching six-packs or several quart bottles of beer. Everyone knows that this is the dangerous hour on the roads outside and inside the vast drinking arena where uniformed bouncers and security men are becoming watchful and tense. In the crowd, a man carrying two jugs of beer brushes by the poised billiard cue of a man drunkenly trying to focus on the ball. A fist flies, beer splashes over a circle of people, a brawl erupts, and the bouncers and police move in.*

These incidents,  and hundreds like them, occur daily in New Zealand. We could equally begin this book with a week's clippings from any local newspaper. No one would question that violent things happen here. But is the daily life of the ordinary New Zealander conducted in some seething turmoil of continuing violence?

In this book we will provide a perspective on the origin and nature, incidence and significance of violence in New Zealand. Almost every kind of violence that occurs elsewhere occurs here, and to read the political press, and the public response, one might be tempted to think that the country is in the grip of forces of violence sweeping it towards a chaos in which personal liberty and safety will be destroyed.

This concern is not new. It is reflected in editorials and correspondence columns of the earliest newspapers published in this country. From the beginning of European settlement, white colonists saw everyone else as a threat to law and order, even at times the imperial army of Her Majesty, Queen Victoria, and Maori leaders were concerned with the increasing numbers of their own kind drawn or thrust into lawlessness.

Many now consider that violence is escalating, that society is breaking down, that the family is falling apart, that the young – especially the young – are subjected to new temptations and influences. People now lock their houses, install property protection devices; some even have firearms under their beds (or say they have). Are such views and actions really justified, or are we fighting our own shadows?

Is there a greater threat to life? The number of murders has certainly risen in recent years but is still only a tenth of road fatalities that occur each and every year. Cigarettes kill far more people each week than are murdered in a year in New Zealand.

Violence is related to a whole range of phenomena: the age distribution of the population; the health of the economy; the social context of control around an individual; the availability of firearms; the development of anti-social groups; the nature of sex roles and gender relationships, our history and institutions.

At the widest level, there are cultural patterns that lie behind the way violence is expressed and against whom. So our task is not only to ask how much violence there is in New Zealand, but also why it takes the pattern and form that it does. Everyone says that they want less. Why has that not happened?

Our aim is to search for linkages, to understand and to evaluate the relationship between known causes so that we can separate myth and folklore from facts. We will be seeking answers to the question: is there anything distinctive about the *patterns* of violence in New Zealand? There are historical factors which make New Zealand different from any other part of the world, and there are beliefs about ourselves of which we must take account. Perhaps we are not really as bland, as assured, and as peaceable as we would like to think we are.

When, as a society, or as individuals, we attempt to deal with one manifestation of the cultural pattern of violence, we are often dismayed to find that our best efforts come to naught. The overall problem remains. Some say that this is because we have not eliminated causes. That may be true. But we will emphasise what Bateson calls 'the pattern that connects', the pattern of cultural assumptions, acceptances, justifications, investments and entrenchments that reinforces the persistence of violence (18).

Both of the major cultures in this country have their own history of violence. They met in violence and, in one form or another, have continued in it ever since. There was the violence of warfare, there was the violence of environmental destruction, and there was a range of domestic, institutional, and legal violence based on primitive permissions, that is, the belief that an individual or group had the right to punish another whether through summary justice or in the heat of an angry altercation.

In this book we will draw together the strands that came from this dark punitive stain which spreads widely through almost every part of the social fabric. It is there in our beliefs about child training; it is there in the way we pattern sex roles, their prescriptions and permissions; it is there in our attitude towards those who would seek possession of what we regard as our property. Remember the old Maori proverb: He wahine, he whenua, kua mate he tangata: It is for women and for land that men will die.

There are connections between sporting violence, family violence, the kind of television we watch, the sort of video we hire, what we do or think we have a right to do with our sexuality (or that of another), the way we use alcohol, the way we drive vehicles, and the sanctions and permissions which apply in all these spheres.

Some years ago, after surveying the phenomena of violence in New Zealand, and the social background, we found it difficult to explain why there was not more violence. We concluded that New Zealand culture limited violence with tight social controls, rigidly applied. We believed this to be the case with parental authority in childhood, and in most other socially imposed patterns of authority or control (198).

Of one thing there is no doubt: the topic of violence provokes strong statements and powerful reactions, many of which are as irrational as violence itself. Violence as a concept is a trigger which releases culturally patterned explanations that are, in themselves, subtly linked with the origins of violence. As we will see, we use a variety of defences to protect ourselves, not so much from violence itself as from the necessity of making life-style changes so basic that they call, in the end, for changes in our national character.

For violence to occur, something or someone must be violated. In previous work we used a straightforward definition of violence as any act which harms another (197). Generally speaking, this means that violence is defined in terms of the victim, regardless of the intention or protestations of goodwill or good intent ('I am only doing this for your own good') by the aggressor.

We place the emphasis of our approach upon the victim, the person who is harmed, and the harm done to them, because the person committing the violence will attempt to deny the act or put it out of consciousness. The perpetrator easily becomes caught up in defences, denials, excuses, permissions, moral sanctions, and role performances that serve well as justifications. Many parents believe they are not performing their duties properly unless they smack their children; how can prison officers not act punitively? That is their job. Many an inadequate teacher will play to the classroom gallery and mock a poor learner.

Individuals are violated when another person takes action against them which has the quality of power or force to induce them to do, or to submit to, something which they would rather not. But we all are caught up, on occasion, in imposing our will upon another person. Is that always violent? In the end, probably yes, but reason must be taken into account. If you can explain to me (without using power) why I should submit to your will, and I agree to do so, then I have not been violated. There are, of course, exceptions. If after all my efforts to explain to you why you should not kill me, you still appear determined to do so, the law says I may use legitimate force to defend myself and I may have to do so, violently. We leave it to the philosopher of ethics to examine the circumstances under which violence might be justified. Our concern is not with the finer points of moral argument or legal defences based on matters of fact, but with those more obvious social situations where the violence is clear and definable.

In most cases, violence is thought of as a physical act, but in this book we will spread the definition much wider to include threats, psychological assaults, and the violence wrought by institutions on individuals or groups of individuals. Sometimes the act of violation is clear, hard and forceful, committed with quite conscious and deliberate intent, but often, only the victim is really aware that violence has occurred – and sometimes, not until later. But in our view, a violent act is a violent act, whether intended or unintended, whether conscious or unconscious, whether direct or hidden, whether physical or psychological.

Some discussions attempt to make distinctions between physical and non-physical violence. Some writers seek to separate expressive violence, that is, the violence which bursts out almost regardless of victim and situation, and instrumental violence, violence which is designed to achieve an end and is therefore used with greater deliberation (235). Not all coercive acts are violent – for example, bribery – but all violent acts are coercive.

To understand violence, therefore, we need to look not only at the act but at the social context in which it occurs, the previous history of the aggressor, and why he (or less frequently, she) chose, or was able to choose, this particular victim. We need to understand why the ordinary processes of social control seem not to apply to this person, or have broken down, or have been discarded on this occasion. We need to understand how, and why, and how often the violent person gets away with it, and the powerful satisfaction that arises when this occurs.

Sometimes a distinction is made between so-called 'normal violence' and 'abusive violence'. Straus, Gelles and Steinmetz, the major American research team working in the area of domestic violence, use this distinction since much domestic violence, as in the spanking of children or the hitting of a spouse, is taken for granted, not only in the family concerned, but also in the neighbourhood (239). Such acts are traditionally regarded as necessary, useful, inevitable, or instinctive. They contrast this with abusive violence, namely, acts in which it is highly likely that someone will suffer physical injury. But in the end, the distinction becomes blurred and they are forced back into the same position that we ourselves adopted in *Spare the Rod*, in which we pointed out that the difference between child abuse and the kind of smack that many parents regard as ordinary discipline may rest on nothing more substantial than whether the child fell against the sharp edge of the table and cracked her skull, or whether she managed to evade the falling hand and run out the door (197).

The range of violent acts is continuous, from shouting at the office junior to bombing an aircraft for terrorist purposes. Of course the two acts are different, but as long as we emphasise the difference we will not see the similarities, nor realise how easily the extremity of violence induces us to respond in kind.

There are two ways in which violent acts become cyclical. One is the inter-generational cycling effect – violence breeds violence. The other is the cycle of stimulus and response that escalates violence towards crisis (105).

Inter-generational violence is not inevitable though the likelihood is great unless intervention changes the whole nexus of frustration, strain, domestic violence, and bad parenting practice (214). We have known for years the circumstances that are likely to produce a high probability of generational replication of behaviour patterns. The term 'at-risk' families may, of itself, be relatively recent, but the phenomenon that it refers to has been around for a long time (233). Rutter and Madge show that where the wheel of fate or some favourable circumstance intervenes, an individual may be switched from the repetition of harmful family patterns into a more socially desirable life-style (214). We did not need social science to tell us this; it is there in the writings of Dickens and in the worthy intentions of the nineteenth-century social reformers.

Knowing that the cycle can be broken is one thing. Marshalling the intervention necessary to produce change is another. Intervention poses such problems of human and social rights that it seems we prefer to allow violent patterns to persist from generation to generation. We know that de-escalation in chains of violent action can be achieved (80). Human relations workshop activities show that individuals can be trained in the skills of de-escalation (166). The problem is that those who most need such training are least likely to obtain it. Many who could use this kind of knowledge and skill are not offered it, even though they could directly employ it in their regular dealings with violent people.

In New Zealand, twenty years ago, an enlightened educator, Garfield Johnson, realised the advantages of human relations training and proposed a curriculum for use in high schools (41). The nature of the curriculum itself was not properly debated in the public arena and was not publicly adopted because a small coterie of vociferous lobbyists combined to implement a strategy of media publicity and political pressure which blocked the adoption of the report (titled, mildly enough, 'Growing, Learning, Sharing'). The young people who would have benefited from this curriculum were then aged fifteen and are now aged thirty. They are becoming parents and perpetuating traditional patterns including crisis escalation and the acting out of violent impulse. It is, perhaps, not unrelated that this past decade has also seen an increase in public violence and violent crime.

As a society, we cannot rely upon sudden revelation, the blinding lightning bolt of insight, or radical conversion, as ways of eliminating violence from our society. We need hard analysis followed by self-examination and hard work. We know that patterns of violent behaviour are learnt and transmitted, and that they can therefore be replaced by other behaviour, or never learned in the first place (13).

# 2
# The Nature of Violence

Our society regards violent propensities as an inevitable part of our nature as human beings. This proposition is considered to be supported and self-evident both by religious fundamentalism and by some scientific evolutionists. But is it necessarily true?

Central to the conservative religious viewpoint is the belief that violence is an expression of original sin. In the Judeo-Christian case, it resulted when Satan induced Eve to offer poor weak-willed Adam the apple in the Garden of Eden, when Cain killed Abel and so on. Other Middle Eastern religions also view violent behaviour as a consequence of the human condition which arose when 'Man' fell from grace and lost 'his' divine quality. Theologies that do not see humanity as fallen from grace do not, generally, place evil inside the person. However modified in modern theology, the doctrine of original sin continues.

Some evolutionists and animal ethologists have similarly concluded that our human origins and therefore our human nature, are 'red in tooth and claw', and that we survived by virtue of our prowess as hunters and fighters (8, 129, 158). From the height of their popularity in the late 1960s, such theories have declined in scientific favour but remain as a kind of popular mythology. As Leakey has pointed out, we did not survive as a species because we were strong and brave and could beat, bully or frighten everything else; we survived because we were small and fleet, because we could eat almost anything that came our way, including the carrion left over by predators, and because we could co-operate both in hunting and in times of hardship (121, 122). We survived not through courage, but through cowardice. The criterion of evolutionary success is the capacity to breed, not to draw blood. We were not the biggest species around – but we were the smartest.

The ethologists were so impressed with animal dominance, display, and territorial behaviour that they seemed to forget that the purpose of these things is not to conquer but to perpetuate the species. If warfare was genetic, the warriors would slowly have extinguished themselves by killing one another. Human beings simply do not carry genetic behaviour patterns for anything so species-threatening as violence or as complicated as warfare. What kind of genetic pattern could apply all the way from hand-to-hand combat with primitive weapons to pressing the button that releases a nuclear bomb? Warfare is a cultural not a genetic trait.

Social scientists have established definite criteria for instinctive behaviour. It must be shown to rely upon a biological, biochemical or hormonal process; it must be shown to have continuity over the evolutionary sequence of development; and it must be found in every culture of which we have knowledge. We shall now discuss these three criteria.

If there is a biological basis for aggression, and therefore for violence, you would expect every individual to be violent unless the biological basis was sex linked, in which case all men would be violent and no woman would be. That this is untrue is self-evident. Frequently, a male propensity for aggression is inaccurately attributed to male hormones (135). There is, however, no such thing as an exclusively male hormone. Both males and females secrete androgens and progesterone. Furthermore, primate studies have shown that hormonal levels vary in terms of the social situation in which the animal may find itself.

Some years ago Rose showed that there was a direct relationship between androgen level and the status hierarchy of a monkey troop, which suggests hormonal control of dominance behaviour (207). However, when lower status monkeys were put in a situation where they could dominate other monkeys, their androgen levels rose dramatically. It is not, therefore, possible to attribute a causal role in dominance behaviour to the male hormone.

The whole relationship between biological processes and behaviour is interactive and complex (156). Those who argue that aggression and violence are instinctive and, therefore, inevitable frequently base their opinions on metaphors drawn from putative animal behaviour and assumptions concerning human evolution which are neither good poetry nor good science. They are, in fact, pernicious because they reinforce the perceived cultural mythology that violent behaviour is part of the human repertoire and thus difficult to change.

Reprehensible as it may be to misinterpret observations of human behaviour, ethological popularists such as Desmond Morris manage to malign animals as well (158). The great cats are not rampaging, violent beasts, but rather slumberous energy conservers who because they prefer fresh meat, make the first strike in the food sequence amongst the meat eaters. Later the carrion eaters, including species descendant from our own progenitors feed on the left-overs. They do not fight amongst themselves except to establish dominance and do not engage in anything comparable to battle or warfare with other prides of lions. Lions are neither peaceable nor warlike; they are just lions and a danger to other species only when specific stimuli induce specific attack behaviours.

Throughout human history, our basic food sources have been nuts, roots, fruits and cereals, and small game animals. The vegetable food sources, traditionally produced or gathered by women, were the most plentiful and reliable. If humanity had had to depend upon man the hunter, we would never have survived. For all the male glorification of inventions such as the bow and arrow, Leakey believes that the invention of the carrying basket and the pottery, gourd or other container – universally made, used, and presumably invented or grown by women – was by far the more significant evolutionary step (122). Women, after all, had to ensure the survival not only of themselves but also of their children.

Even the myth that men are predisposed to dominance or territorial behaviour does not stand up under close scrutiny. Of the forty-two studies reviewed by Maccoby and Jacklin which examined sex differences in dominance behaviour, only fifteen showed clear evidence of male dominance, and a number of these used measures of dominance heavily saturated with cultural assumptions concerning male behaviour (135). Twenty-seven (60 per cent) of the studies showed no evidence of greater male dominance. This result may seem surprising in the light of cultural mythologies, but men have a vested interest in maintaining the myths.

One cross-cultural study showed that girls were more likely than boys to attempt to control the behaviour of others in the interests of the social group or the welfare of the individual, whereas boys make more attempts at egotistic dominance (255).

Territorial behaviour occurs in human groups only when there is pressure on resources. Characteristically, the human species have been migratory range dwellers; even when settled into agriculture, we shifted with it in order to sustain soil fertility. We move on. Narrowly defined territorial attachment is not part of our genetic history, but becomes important when small bands are locked into a limited territory by others. This is as true of the highlands of New Guinea as it is of the gang territories of the San Fernando Valley, the streets of New York, or the suburbs of South Auckland. When the territorial argument is applied to humans it reinforces beliefs about the inherent nature of violence which is socially determined (and therefore capable of change) rather than biologically prescribed.

The ethologists also emphasise a bestial and predatory view of sex that has little to do with the actual nature of human sexuality. The biological fact that has produced evolutionary success for the human species has been the capacity to perform sexually anywhere, at any time, with anyone, over and over again, with a high likelihood of impregnation. If this is what Desmond Morris means when he describes us as the sexiest mammals around, we would agree, but the human species is not characterised by high levels of sexual desire nor strength of sexual urge (158). Furthermore, there is no evidence to show that human males have greater sexual need or capacity than females; indeed, recovery after orgasm is more rapid in the female (141). The myths about rapacious male sexuality we believe to be based upon greater male sexual insecurity. The link between male violence and male sexuality is psychologically and socially real, but is not biologically determined.

Violence, then, is not a genetically encoded part of either human nature or male nature, although it is traditionally associated with both. Later, we will look at the ways in which this association is built up by cultural expectations and permissions. When we look for evolutionary linkages, it should not be unexpected that we do not find them. Present primate species are mostly peaceable unless provoked or under pressure. Past progenitors, as already indicated, were probably too busy surviving to spend much time making either love or war.

So much, then, for the criteria of a biological basis and evolutionary continuity. What about cross-cultural universality in violent behaviour? Were we simply logic-chopping, we would need to produce just one culture in which there is no violence for the argument to be destroyed. There are, in fact, many cultures in which gentleness, mildness, peaceableness, persuasion, co-operation, caring, nurturance, and similar values predominate. 'Make love, not war' is not simply a graffiti slogan which emerged in the late 1960s, but has been the basis of advance and development in many human societies. Indeed, even in our own culture, where violence is so frequent a phenomenon, there is a charter ethic against it.

The cross-cultural record shows that although violence is embedded in some aspects of some cultures it is not uniformly present, and that even rape, so often presumed to be universal and inevitable, is found in only 53 per cent of the human societies for which evidence is available (218). Although Brownmiller says that 'when men discovered that they could rape they proceeded to do it' in order to 'keep all women in a constant state of intimidation' (30:209), rape was rare or absent in 47 per cent of the 156 human societies which Sanday studied. This study seems to suggest that human societies fall on either side of a watershed. While violence can occur anywhere, there are societies where it is frequent, and societies where it is infrequent. On one side of the ridge live the tribe who glorify courage and stamina, who delight in victory, who idealise the warrior and other forms of male supremacy, and who mistreat, beat and rape women. In such tribes, men as a social group are generally pitched against women and against one another. Property is emphasised, as is competition in all things including economic exchange, and the exclusive possession by men of women and children who are regarded as male dependents. Only in emergencies do men in such societies put the welfare of women and children first (72).

In Sanday's rape-free societies there is less emphasis on violence of any kind and a greater respect for individual feelings. Decisions are made by common consent, sex-role divisions are blurred, and there is a greater respect for nature and natural processes with a frequent linkage of the earth, women, blood, and sexuality. The tribe who live on this side of the watershed simply do not have any place in their life-style for violent behaviour. On those rare occasions when it does occur, the perpetrator is excluded and becomes a non-person, even to the point of invisibility.

The classic study in this area is Margaret Mead's report of three tribes living along the course of the Sepik River in New Guinea (142). The Arapesh who lived in the highland upreaches of the river knew of warfare because their territorial neighbours engaged in it and occasionally forced them to participate in it, but it was rarely and reluctantly undertaken and had no value for individuals in the society. Amongst the Arapesh any kind of fighting or altercation was shameful. Men and women shared child rearing and acted in nurturant ways toward each other. Rape was unknown, the accumulation of personal property was not valued, and the energy of the tribe was directed at survival in a rugged and difficult environment. Surrounded as they were by aggressors, the Arapesh had come to value non-aggression above almost everything else.

Down in the middle reaches of the Sepik lived the Mundugamor, fierce, cannibalistic, competitive, harsh in their treatment of both women and children, and suspicious and paranoid in their social interactions. The relative ease of their life on the river plains contrasted with the poverty of the mountain Arapesh, but there was a heavy round of food-producing labour, largely done by the women, which made their life very dreary. As they paddled through the swampy waterways they had to be wary of enemies and natural dangers such as crocodiles and snakes. But there was no sense of banding together in common protection against a common danger. Fathers and sons competed for wives, since wives were obtained by daughter/sister exchange, and polygamy enabled a father to have many wives at his son's expense. Public displays of affection were considered shameful, and infants spent their days strung up in rigid bark baskets, away from human contact. Even breast-feeding was harsh and cruel; mothers fed hastily, standing up, and if the child coughed or spluttered, it was rapidly removed from the breast. Sexual violence was common.

In the lower Sepik, on the coastal reaches of the flood plain, lies a lake called Tchambuli where the food resources were greater and were supplemented and varied by extensive patterns of trade. Here it was the men who dressed up and went to market with the food and other trade goods that were produced (largely by the women). Marketing was regarded simply as another of the many dramatic arenas in which men performed. The men preened, made up their faces and attended to their dress, gossiped and engaged in backbiting and verbal hostility, while the women, briskly businesslike, carried on with child rearing, food production, and the political affairs of the village.

Slightly to the north lived a related group, the Iatmul, similar in many respects to the Tchambuli, but among whom rituals of role reversal, called Naven, occurred from time to time. In Naven ceremonies the women were, for a time, dominant, made sexual advances to the men, and imitated their grandiose behaviour in a kind of burlesque, while the men slipped quietly into the provider role, characteristic of women. It was the role, not the gender, which endorsed dominance, assertiveness, and aggression (17).

Erik Fromm, in an important cross-cultural study, produced a typology with three categories of society (72). The first are those which are life-affirming, in which destructiveness, combativeness, and any kind of belligerence are abjured. The gentle Pueblo societies of the American southwest, described by Ruth Benedict in her book *Patterns of Culture*, are cultures whose prevailing ethic is to live a harmonious life close to natural patterns and rhythms, to be calm, to be contemplative, and to avoid disruption (24). In the anthropological literature there are many more societies of this kind. Almost all the hunting and gathering societies were like this. Warfare is a human luxury which those who live by subsistence can rarely afford. We need go no further than our own history to find groups which adopted a non-violent ethic and lived by it. The people of Parihaka (181) and the Moriori (112) both adopted pacifist strategies.

Fromm's second type of society achieves creation through destruction. Its ethic is one of renewal which is then ritualised ceremonially. The Hawaiians ritually sacrificed in ceremonies of seasonal renewal; the Kwakiutl of the Vancouver coast celebrated their affluence by great ceremonies called potlatch, in which they feasted on, gifted, and destroyed their material wealth. The American and Soviet space race is really potlatch behaviour, as is a cocktail party, in that both involve the consumption or destruction of property to show one's prestige. In such societies, status enhancement tends to incorporate elements of arrogance, pride, exhibitionism, and display.

Fromm's third type of society has a central dedication to patterns of destruction which appear to be unstoppable. Examples of such patterns are the exploitation of the environment and the nuclear arms race.

Fromm argues that destructive societies inculcate the kind of character traits that are necessary in order to transform a rather defenceless, cowardly, small mammal into the most destructive species the world has ever seen. The tool that achieves this transformation is the power complex which includes the ideology of retribution, punishment, and asserting a right to dominate and control. This ideology creates a norm of violence. This means not that everyone acts violently but that violence is accepted as a normal part of human nature. We can then excuse, both in ourselves and in others, the inexcusable.

It has been said of the anthropological record that you can pick any kind of society that you want depending on the point you wish to make. But it is this very variety which makes *our* point. High levels of violence are associated with egocentric values, self-seeking environmental exploitation, and sharp sex-role and other status differentiations. Violence is highly likely in a society where some are enslaved (whether by gender, race or class) and where equality is denied.

What some call our 'human nature' has in fact been determined by human history, which has led us away from genetically defined behaviour patterns to become the species that learns. The process of achieving upright stature required physical adaptions in the foetus and in mother-child dependency in order to secure survival. The consequences of these physical changes are that each of us is born in such a state of neural incompleteness or foetal immaturity that we spend nearly a quarter to a third of our natural lifespan becoming mature. In this process, instinctive behavioural patterns have been lost and replaced by the generalised neural capacity to learn, to modify, and to adapt which continues throughout our lives.

Certain patterns of behaviour predominate because they are

learned early and so block other patterns, and because they are massively reinforced by repeated messages from many different agencies in our lives. We are not violent because of television, or what our mothers or fathers did to us, or because we were taught to fear a punitive God, or are forced to live in an atmosphere of 'dog eats dog' (another myth, and most unfair to dogs!). Nor is it because our country calls us to fight in a foreign field, or because we are male or female. It is because all our cultural agencies repeat the same message – violence is the way we are. In the last analysis, we regard our own nature as violent and make this the excuse to tolerate violence in ourselves and in others. We are violent because we will not use our most human capacity – the capacity to change – to eliminate violent cultural patterns.

# 3

# The Psychology of Violence

The psychology of violence attempts to answer three questions. What is the general nature of violence – that is, how does it arise as a general human propensity? What are the conditions that increase that propensity in some, rather than others? And what are the motivational patterns that lie behind particular forms of violent expression?

It is a curious fact that, although violent behaviour is quite common in our society and causes so much public concern, it has been relatively neglected by the social sciences in general, and psychology in particular. In the 1930s, with one world war past, and another imminent, more attention was given to violence. Similarly, after World War II, the UNESCO Tensions Project sought ways of reducing international conflict (252). It focused on improving international understanding and reducing racial hatred, and attempted to understand the psychology of authoritarian regimes and leadership. While none of these laudable but grandiose aims was fulfilled, the project did contribute a little to our understanding.

Many years ago, Clark Hull suggested that any kind of behaviour could be regarded as having four phases (101). First, there is a pre-existing state which Hull called the *drive* condition. For example, the businessman who leaves home to get into his car and drive to work is in a very different condition from the man who, having spent the evening at the pub, comes home, quarrels with his wife, and then drives off dangerously into the night. If overtaken by another motorist driving faster, their reactions are likely to be different. Drive states depend upon a variety of prior conditions, some of a very general nature, such as temperament, and others more specific to the moment, such as blood sugar level and fatigue. Drive conditions affect readiness to act and a greater propensity for one kind of behaviour rather than another: for example, hunger leads to food seeking, rather than to sexual activity.

The second phase develops when a *cue* or stimulus focuses the drive state on a particular goal. Now things begin to move. The motivated individual begins to ignore other signals and seeks only the desired end. Behaviour becomes more efficient, more selective, narrower. The third step is, therefore, the *response* itself which, if it achieves the goal, is more likely to occur next time the individual is similarly motivated. This final phase, the consequences which attend or follow the act, is called *reinforcement*.

This rather simplified drive-cue-response-reinforcement sequence is quite useful in analysing simple behaviour, but inevitably the paradigm is hard to apply to more complex human events. However, it does focus attention upon the fact that smooth chains of non-violent behaviour will lead to satisfaction and produce satisfied individuals who have no need to act disruptively. However, a violent response where the intention is to be violent also achieves its goal and reinforces the violent pattern.

In 1941 psychologists Miller and Dollard suggested that the disruption of such chains might be a likely source of aggression (146, 147). They first formulated the now famous frustration-aggression hypothesis. This states that when an individual is prevented from reaching a goal, aggression results. This simple, clear notion seems self-evident, yet in the series of studies that followed to test it, the outcome was by no means clearcut. Some studies confirmed the hypothesis (120) but others did not (75). Human beings can defer their gratifications and can deal with delays without anger, yet in sheer probability terms, the hypothesis (even if hedged around with all sorts of qualifications) seemed to have more than a grain of truth.

In general, people whose lives subject them to many and severe frustrations, are more likely to feel hostile and deprived. These feelings may. either lead to violent outbursts or be reflected inwards to produce feelings of incompetence, a poor self-image, depression or even suicide. What we might call, for want of a better term, anger-because-of-one's-circumstances, may be directed outwards or inwards.

The hypothesis has had an interesting public reaction. It acted as a stimulus for hostile comment from those who saw psychology as a pernicious proponent of moral decline. We know of no psychologist who said 'do not frustrate activity for fear of the consequences', although that is the interpretation which many social commentators put upon it. The frustration-aggression hypothesis says nothing about public policy and criminals and their victims. It simply says that the disruption of the chains of behaviour that lead to satisfaction produces a negative situation, one consequence of which is aggression. It says nothing about what happens next. Nor does it tell us much about who is likely to be violent, where, when, in what way, and towards whom. It certainly does little to explain either violent assault or rape.

There were similar misinterpretations of the real messages that were coming from Freudian psychology (69). The truth is that Freud was in favour of strengthening social control rather than advocating unbridled licence. In his social writings Freud clearly expressed his belief that both sex and anger could be powerfully disruptive of the social order, and in his instinct theory he argued that the power of these two 'forces' had to be captured or sublimated for the social good. He saw art, literature, and science as substitutes for both the erotic and the destructive capacities of human beings, and would certainly have agreed with those ethologists who believe in the erroneous notion that somewhere within us there is a native beast that society must tame (70).

On the whole, we do not think that Freudian psychology provided much illumination in this matter, and in one respect it compounded the problem by popularising the notion of cathexis as the investment and build-up of emotional energy on a desired object until, in catharsis, that energy is released. Freud borrowed this idea (as he did so much else) from the dramatic themes of Greek theatre. Aristotle thought a really good play should begin by building up a momentum, an energy, an excitement (cathexis) until, at some critical point, this energy was discharged either with great dramatic intensity or in a controlled development (catharsis), leaving the audience satisfied that the tension which had been created was finally resolved.

Freud's corresponding notion was that a desired, but un-attainable, objective becomes the focus of psychic energy which would build to a crisis and then be discharged either positively (eros equals construction) or negatively (thanatos equals destruction). Freud used this concept to show how individuals can come to kill the objects of their love, or come to love those whom they might, perhaps, more rationally have hated (70). In the complexities of psychopathology, such reversals are not uncommon, but this is a peculiar matter. We do not all act this way.

In psychoanalysis the process of cathexis was supposed to be therapeutically useful in encouraging the patient to transfer onto the therapist all the feelings of love and hate that had been built up during childhood. The crisis in therapy would come when this emotional load was discharged. Freud believe this led to insight into the process, but cathartic therapy got going under its own steam and left insight and reason a long way behind. A whole range of cathartic cults grew up in which play therapists encouraged children to beat up dolls, and people in encounter groups were encouraged to get rid of their feelings by whacking one another with bean bags and cushions. Catharsis came to mean engaging in unrestricted expression of an emotion in order to clear it from one's system. But does it work?

The psychology of this is a little murky. Even in the management of grief, emotional release does not guarantee recovery. Rather, it is the working through of stages of development, the learning of adaptions to the new situation, that are emphasised in the work of people such as Kubler-Ross (117, 118).

The Freudian notion of catharsis has become a justification for indulging in one form of violence as a substitute for another, or for purveying violence in the market-place as having some sort of preventive social benefit. For example, heavy action sport such as rugby is encouraged as a kind of social emetic for violent behaviour. Were this the case, rugby players would all be the mildest of men off the field. Some are, some are not. The theory is not only nonsense, it may even be pernicious. The action of catharsis encourages that which it is supposed to eliminate. The rewards at the end of the behaviour chain may make it more likely that the behaviour will be repeated.

Allowing people to act aggressively lowers their threshold for aggressive acts (74). Instead of the reservoir of potential aggression being emptied, so to speak, the channel for aggressive behaviour is deepened, widened, and opened. The notion that healthy young men should be allowed to engage in socially sanctioned violent behaviour in order to make them less violent is not psychologically plausible, however widely it may be believed in our society. If we want to reduce violent behaviour, we must simply stop encouraging violent activities.

Nor does observing violence reduce the likelihood that we will act violently. The evidence is, overwhelmingly, the reverse. The more violent the sports event, the more likely it is that there will be spectator violence also (82). Watching violence increases the level of arousal, and whether this spills over into active violence depends on whether the individual is cued to release aggressive responses.

Every step in the chain with which we began can be subject to modification: that is, we can teach individuals greater control at each phase.

The state of arousal which leads to violent behaviour can be recognised, and individuals can learn ways of dealing with the arousal other than by acting aggressively. Simply to recognise that one is on the track to a higher level of arousal than one can contain can short-circuit the sequence. Individuals can learn to 'read' their state and stop right there.

All of us know the personal cues, the stimuli which will bring our anger to flash-point. We may not know how to deal with those cues in non-violent ways. Simply to go through the exercise of listing all the annoying things that have occurred in the last twenty-four hours is helpful. Once we know that we are likely to be provoked by an action, person or situation, we can warn ourselves and others if we are unable to take evasive action by leaving the field.

Learning alternative response patterns may be difficult, but responses that strengthen control are more sane, more civilised, and more sensible, and are, therefore, more likely to meet with social rewards. Displaying angry reactions may also increase our vulnerability by giving others information about our points of provocation.

Anger and violence can be demonstrations that an individual is searching for power, not that they possess it. Such violence is, therefore, not a sign of strength, but a display of weakness. Violent acts are often a response to some threat or inadequacy, and always relate to power relationships. It is easy enough to see how a small, weak, inadequate person deprived of power might seek it, but, if this were the only explanation, women would be more violent and men less. The problem is to explain why the person who apparently has power seeks to exercise it, and to do so in ways which risk the security of dominating. For example, when a man beats his wife there is always a risk that she will walk out, but it is also likely that the act of wife-beating reinforces the woman's powerlessness, making it less likely that she will leave.

The anthropological record shows that those who have the greatest guarantee of power, such as hereditary chiefs, do not need recourse to violence of a personal kind, although in many such societies ritualised and institutionalised violence may be directed against females or performed in ceremonial rites of passage (138). If the rich and powerful want to act oppressively, they usually get someone else to do it for them. They have no need to be personally violent. It is, more often, insecure individuals, who, having clawed their way up to a position of power, maintain it with violence. They learn to use the tactics of intimidation, the marketing of fear, the generation of strong in-group loyalty and strong out-group hostility, and all the other tricks of the power trade.

No political system can be free from the danger of those who seek power as over-compensation for personal inadequacy. Hitler, after all, was democratically elected; Napoleon was fiercely popular. History would have been less dramatic and colourful, but also a lot less bloody, were it not for the little men who made big.

The psychologist who understood this best was 5 feet 4 inches tall and his name was Alfred Adler (2). He had to establish his psychology against the dominating personality of Sigmund Freud. In Adler's view, every human being was subject to the anxieties that arise from inadequacy. We are not always successful, and when we fail we may find it hard to accept. Our imagination builds aspirations which we may have neither the energy nor the skills to achieve. We are, after all, rather puny mammals who happen to have big heads. We grow for years surrounded by people who are bigger and more powerful than we are as children. We begin life dependent, and must struggle for independence.

For all these reasons, as well as the added load of cultural conditioning and bad models, Adler thought we were all destined to become power seekers. Adler believed that, because of the threat this constituted to order and humanity, human beings were taught to have a will to community which offset their will to power. He saw individual psychology as a struggle between these two wills; more in some individuals than in others, because of the personal circumstances which contributed to imbalance; more in some societies, cultures and social circumstances than in others, because of the degree of philosophic reflection on history that could contribute social wisdom; more in one gender than the other, because of the patterning of socialisation and differences in role modelling (2).

Adler's psychology directs us to attend to both the circumstances and the context of growing up. The psychology of oppression can clearly be understood in these terms as well as in the more usual terms of neo-Marxist theory. But remember that there are two aspects to Adler's theories about personal power and violence: personal inadequacy arising from the experience of oppression or failure, and socialisation which transforms will to power into will to community.

The heyday of Adlerian psychology was the inter-war period when Western societies were seeking to formulate the profession of social work and to attend to some of the nastier consequences of urban industrial capitalism. Adler's was a psychology that appealed to social reformers and to those of Christian sentiment; from it you could develop a charter to address crucial issues such as deprivation, unemployment, bad health, and iniquitous or inequitable class distinction, and improve education to reduce failure and emphasise the study of society, in the hope that some new dawn would arise through the practice of applied Christianity and social work.

The idealism of such social policy deserves neither scorn nor admiration. It did, after all, rise out of the slums of Chicago and similar cities, where middle- and upper-class reformers teamed up with academics to provide a whole range of new developments, such as the profession of social work, the study of sociology, and the development of social programmes in public policy (45).

More realistic were the social thinkers in the tradition of the London School of Economics who insisted that something more than merely tinkering with problems was required, since the ills of society were not based on individual psychopathology but upon the structural inequities in the distribution of resources and power (179). Those who control wealth, control people, and allocate opportunity. Thus the weakness in the Adlerian scheme is that individual psychology is not enough. Power is not just a matter of personal reaction against perceived or unconscious inadequacy, but is about the opportunities for ease and comfort and extending one's control over people and things.

Whatever the origins of one's will to power, the psychologist Gordon Allport believed that it became, to use his jargon, functionally autonomous, that is, intrinsically rewarding or reinforcing (5). Thus, long after an individual has escaped from being bullied and dominated by his father, he may also bully and dominate because, by doing so, he has the satisfaction of seeing others cower. Such satisfactions may become central postulates in cults of violence such as gang rituals, martial arts cults or other male hierarchical structures.

Up to this point, we have tried to deal with the general background of violent behaviour. But this does not provide an adequate account of why some individuals are given to assault, some to rape and sexual abuse, and some to domestic violence. We will take up these matters as we discuss the phenomena of violence in the following two chapters.

But before we do so we need to address the question of how violent behaviour comes, in some circumstances, to receive social approval.

When the Nazi holocaust rolled over central Europe and the liberal centres of social reform, many Jewish intellectuals were forced to leave their homelands for refuge in countries which they believed would be free from fascism (20). They found, of course, that fascism is everywhere and that the true price of freedom is, indeed, eternal vigilance.

One of them, Kurt Lewin, became the founder of social psychology. He turned from abstract psychological theory and devoted all his energies to an extraordinary series of applied social studies, all of which centred on revealing the roots of anti-semitism and contrasting autocratic and democratic leadership styles (126). Lewin, himself an unlikely ideologue, dramatically demonstrated how leadership ideologies influenced, indeed drastically changed, the behaviour of followers. In one of his studies of boys' clubs a switch from democratic leadership to fascist domination resulted in behaviours we associate with the Nazi brownshirts and the Gestapo. Dominance hierarchies were established, with downward pecking order, scapegoating, and victimisation, and led to a general upsurge of overt displays of aggression. Some boys simply crumbled and became the submissive victims of others.

Another migrant, the psychotherapist Karen Horney, found her training in psychoanalysis inappropriate for her client problems in the United States, where neurosis seemed to be caused more often by interpersonal hostility and feelings of anger, aggression and violence suppressed or expressed, than by sexual difficulties (97). She had expected American democracy to be benign. In terms of social expression it was, but at the personal level the fascist urge was appallingly prevalent.

Before leaving Europe, a group of socialist and Marxist reformers, the so-called Vienna circle, had already been critically examining the basis of political power and control in modern Western societies. When they came to America their work took off in different directions, but from that common base. Erik Fromm, in his pioneering study, *Fear of Freedom*, argued that, as we approach true liberty, the challenge to traditional securities produces anxiety and panic, and we may resort to repressive mechanisms in order to protect ourselves from these insecurities. We fear freedom because we fear the responsibilities which it might bring: no one to blame, no one to shelter behind, no one to make the decisions. You are free, but lonely and alone (71). Fromm was later to make many statements about viciousness, destructiveness, and the dark and violent side of human nature (72).

Further pioneering work on the ideology of violence was done by other members of the Vienna circle, including Adorno, Frenkel-Brunswick and others who, in a series of studies, explored the authoritarian personality (3). When this work became public in the early 1950s, it produced an energetic response from social scientists but had relatively little public impact. People were too busy breeding, and exploiting post-war affluence, to worry much about a bunch of Jewish expatriates who had disturbing things to say about the similarities between American social attitudes and the political ideologies which had just devastated Europe, killing 20 million people, 6 million of them Jews.

However, their book *The Authoritarian Personality*, stands as one of the great classics of research literature on violence (3). Its core is simply this. Those who are dominated seek to dominate others. If they succeed, they perpetuate the cycle. If they fail, they become submissive to those who succeed in dominating them, and thus they too perpetuate the pattern. Some are socialised to submission from the outset. The authoritarian personality is the personal expression of an authoritarian system. The interlock is deadly and resilient.

The book contained psychoanalytic studies of individuals, studies of the family background of authoritarian personalities, and studies of their habits of mind such as perceptual rigidity and unwillingness to accept new information that might force a change in perspective. Authoritarians use language punctuated by words such as 'surely', 'of course', 'doubtless', 'clearly'. They do not enquire, they assert. They do not discuss, they argue. They do not defend, they attack. They use psychological tactics of belittlement, *ad hominem* argument, shaming, and ridicule. You have met them. They claim that everything they do is rationally based but, when challenged, their irrationality strikes out.

What happened to the notion of the authoritarian personality? To some degree it became part of the common core of social analysis, but a subsequent welter of social science discussion about methodology tended to avoid confronting the unpalatable social reality that Adorno and Frenkel-Brunswick and the rest had exposed. The lesson to be learnt was too painful, the naked nerve too sensitive. And before New Zealanders say of such unpleasant truths that 'it cannot happen here', we should look at some facts about our own attitudes.

*Violence in New Zealand*

# 4

# Violence at Home

While domestic violence in New Zealand does not rage unchecked, it is virtually impossible to obtain any reliable indication of its extent or frequency. The conventional mythology maintains that the family scene is, and has always been, a haven of peace and happiness. But for many it is not, and never was.

Indeed, one might view the family as an arena where personal tensions can be released, but also contained so that they do not spill over into other situations. That does not always happen. A businessman, say, may leave the house after a violent argument in which his teenage children sided with his wife against him, and then take his resentment out on his employees at work. Steinmetz and Straus point out that though we all want to consider child abuse, wife beating, and drunken brawls to be exceptions to the usually placid course of family life, their actual frequency makes them very common exceptions indeed (235). Domestic violence is a daily phenomenon, as any police watch house or women's refuge can testify.

Gelles has shown why the family is so likely to be an arena for violent expression (77). First, family members spend a lot of time at home – women more than men, young people more than older ones – but all may interact more with each other than with anyone else. Families are impacted, enclosed in intense relationships to which the members may be so committed as to feel totally confined. Often the goodies are not equally distributed; money certainly is not, nor are less tangible but no less desirable things such as parental time and attention, love, and, for this discussion, importantly, power.

Belonging to a family gives a person privileged permission to speak personally and directly to and exert influence over other members in ways that usually occur in no other social groups. Most other groups have greater uniformity of membership and are voluntary – you can leave. The age differences in a family may be great and membership is not optional – you cannot move in and out as you please. Roles are assigned on the basis of fixed status rather than interest in or competence for the task. There is no more private institution than the family. Within its walls, insulated from the eyes and ears of prying outsiders, not only are intimate scenes enacted and personal dramas played, but the rules, of both expression and prohibition, may be very different from those outside and provide licence acceptable nowhere else.

Then there is the matter of access to personal histories, which within the family are wide open and their owners vulnerable. No one else can wound as sharply or deeply as kin. The characteristics of grandparents or even more remote family members may be foisted onto their descendants, who may be far from pleased to have Uncle Walter's less pleasant foibles held up as genetic warnings of a dark career ahead. There is a lot of blaming within family relations and justified or not, there is not always much that anyone can do to correct for past actions.

Finally, there is stress. No other social institution is required to stand as much stress from so many sources and with so little outside aid or means of dispersing, displacing or dispelling it. There is not only the stress of personality clashes and daily frustrations, but of major life events and transitions such as a new job, a new house, a birth, the death or departure of a spouse, a child leaving home, financial disasters – everything.

There have been many attempts to measure family stress. Straus, Gelles and Steinmetz developed a useful 18-item scale for their survey of family violence in the USA, and then related the scores to child abuse, spouse abuse and other aspects of family violence. The association is quite direct – the higher the stress score, the more frequent the violence (239).

Having children is stressful for everyone. Difficult, handicapped or otherwise abnormal children certainly compound normal stress, but even normal stress is very great, often over long periods of time. It also may be unequally borne and not expected or accepted. Because the family is a system, the stress of one person frequently becomes the stress of all and the build-up can be intense, rapid, and violent.

In 1981 we surveyed 300 Hamilton adults on their attitudes to the use of force in various situations – family, school, self-defence in the home, the sporting arena (187). We were generally surprised at the high level of endorsement given by our respondents to the use of physical force as a social control. Only 26 per cent of Swedes in the 1970s endorsed the right of a parent to hit a child as a form of discipline, but in our Hamilton survey we found that 86 per cent of the women and 92 per cent of the men found this practice acceptable. Four per cent of the men but only 1 per cent of the women found it acceptable for a parent actually to beat a child (as opposed to slapping), and the same proportion agreed that a spouse could beat his or her partner. Of these, about 25 per cent of the men and about 13 per cent of the women endorsed the right of a spouse to slap a partner's face.

As our child-rearing studies (185, 192) had shown a high level of physical punishment by parents of young children (in our most recent study (191) only 4 per cent of the mothers had never hit their four-year-old child), we were not surprised that so many parents endorsed the practice. But what did surprise us was the high percentage (61 per cent of men, 35 per cent of women) who found it acceptable for a father to hit a teenage son. Interestingly, fewer (48 per cent of men, 28 per cent of women) found it acceptable for a father to hit a teenage daughter.

There was also a high level of approval for the use of corporal punishment in both primary and secondary schools. At the primary level, 65 per cent of men and 36 per cent of women were in favour of corporal punishment in the case of boys; slightly fewer (52 per cent of men, 30 per cent of women) favoured it for girls. At the secondary level, the double standard again applied. More men (62 per cent) and women (29 per cent) endorsed the use of corporal punishment on a boy than on a girl; this was acceptable to only 45 per cent of men and 15 per cent of women (187).

Apart from the general high levels of acceptance of the use of physical force, one of the most interesting patterns detectable in this research was the marked gender difference. Except for areas where there was a very high level of endorsement, such as a parent's right to hit a child, or very low levels of endorsement, such as in the case of a woman beating her partner, men were significantly more likely than women to endorse the use of physical force in solving human problems.

Men were also more likely to have had direct personal experience of violence than women. They were more likely to have been hit by their fathers during their teenage years, to have been hit at secondary school, and to have experienced pub brawls and street fights. Men who had played rugby after leaving school had a generally higher endorsement of violence than those who had not.

In 1988 the attitudes study was repeated in Hamilton with a small sample of 100 adults (202). Similar trends emerged. Once again, men were more likely than women to endorse the use of physical punishment as a way of resolving human conflict and were more likely to have had violent experiences.

There was a slight drop in the number endorsing a parent's right to hit a child, but more men (15 per cent, up from 4 per cent) endorsed the right of a parent to thrash a child, compared to 2 per cent of women (up from 1 per cent). Three per cent of men still found it acceptable for a spouse to beat a partner (compared to 4 per cent in 1981). Though the number of men who endorsed the use of violence with teenage children dropped, almost half of the men still found it acceptable for a father to hit his teenage son, a view held by less than a quarter of the women.

In their 1980 national survey in the United States, Straus, Gelles and Steinmetz asked 2,000 couples how often, in the past year, they had engaged in a violent act towards each other (239). Sixteen per cent, or one in six, of the individuals had committed a violent act against his or her partner in the past year, but over the course of the marriage the figure rose to 28 per cent. By 1985, when the study was repeated, there had been a slight drop in wife abuse (238).

In New Zealand, a team of Otago University researchers surveyed 2,000 women and found that 16 per cent of them had been hit at least once by their male partner (161). Although only two of the women admitted to being subjected to physical abuse at the time of the survey, over half of those hit had been assaulted at least three times. Further New Zealand data is scarce. A team of investigators has been following the development of 1,265 children who were born in Christchurch in 1977. Eight and a half per cent of the mothers in this sample reported one or more assaults from their husband or partner over a two-year period. The investigators consider that this figure is likely to be under-reported because of feelings of shame or guilt (60). Straus and his co-workers make the same point in respect of their much higher figures. They also note that some domestic violence may go under-reported because it is so much a part of normal family life that it is simply not considered noteworthy or even remembered (239).

In their Christchurch study of young families, Fergusson and his colleagues found that factors associated with wife assault were extreme youth of the husband, marriage because of pregnancy, unplanned pregnancies during the marriage, poor education, and no religious affiliation (60). All these factors have been found in overseas studies as well, and indicate that marriages based on necessity or where there is an inability to avoid pregnancy are likely to be more violent.

In the American study by Straus and his associates, throwing, pushing, shoving, and slapping constituted the most frequent violent acts, with kicking, beating up with a fist, or the use of knives or weapons being much less frequent. Nevertheless, hitting, punching or kicking occurred in 5 per cent of couples and about the same percentage reported that they were hit with an instrument. Actual beatings occurred in over 2 per cent of cases in the year before the survey. Over the period of the marriage, the figures were: kicking and punching, 10 per cent; hitting with instrument, 10 per cent; beating up 6 per cent; and use, or threatened use, of a knife or gun, 4 per cent. The authors describe these statistics of heavy violence as 'astoundingly high'. Furthermore, the rates for violence by women were slightly higher than those for men. This is surprising since men have traditionally been considered more aggressive and violent than women. One explanation is that much violence is mutual: 49 per cent of the violence occurred in relationships where both partners were violent. However, men inflict more damage than women and are more likely to use weapons; women are more likely to be acting in self-defence and to use verbal abuse (239).

The natural history of violence within the family is not well documented, but there is evidence that, once a seriously violent incident occurs, the likelihood of further incidents is very high (36, 37). Although some marriages may continue for years without a further violent incident, most violent marriages were that way from the very beginning. In the Straus study, 47 per cent of the couples reported three or more violent incidents in the past year. The highest frequency of beatings usually occurred later in the relationship.

There are a number of popular beliefs which the research evidence does not support (76, 163). Wife beating is not most common amongst the young and immature. In the Gelles study the peak rate for violence occurred in the 40–50 age group as both partners were approaching the transitions of middle age. For the men, the stresses at this time arise mostly from job frustration, occupational entrapment or unfulfilled life goals. Whatever he expected from marriage and family status, the reality may be very different. Now he is confronted with settling for that reality, or making a radical transition. Next to late adolescence, this is the most dangerous age for men.

Women approaching middle age are trapped in even more restrictive ways. Their child-rearing role may be over, leaving, for some, great empty spaces in their lives. If they fill these spaces with other occupations and are even moderately successful, this may exacerbate the insecurities of their partner. Some women become spouse abusers at this time, but many more become victims.

It is sometimes said that spouse beating is found everywhere and bears no relation to education, occupation or income. The evidence

is against this (76, 239). Generally it is concluded that in domestic
situations, the more education, the less violence. There are, however,
two exceptions to this which we must emphasise. Firstly, in the
Straus study, the highest incidence of violence by men towards their
partners was not by those who had no education at all, but was by
those who had some high school education but did not complete it.
Secondly, domestic violence by men continued even at the highest
levels of education.

There are two inconsistent but popular views concerning the
relationship between domestic violence and occupational status, the
commonest being that violence is exclusively a lower-class
phenomenon and the other being that it is found equally in all
occupational levels. Neither assumption is completely true but both
have some validity. Violence is present in every occupational class,
but it is not equally distributed among them. The significant factor
is not the nature of the job itself, but how stressful it is for the
person involved. Where there is competition to keep the job, fear of
redundancy, doubt over one's capacity to perform, or no job at all,
the associated stress may erupt in domestic violence. As a category,
people who are unemployed are at great risk, but the highest risk is
associated with part-time employment (239).

If there is a tendency to violence within a marriage, it frequently
erupts during pregnancy. Many of the men who beat their wives did
not do so until pregnancy had occurred. An unwelcome pregnancy
constitutes a trap to the male: it occurs beyond the individual's
control and is therefore a threat to his autonomy; the woman is
often blamed for her failure to take adequate contraceptive
precautions; and a teetering marriage is brought to the edge of the
precipice. Add to this the possibility of the husband's sexual
deprivation and jealousy of the new-born child and you have a
dangerous combination. The husband no longer has the exclusive
possession of or right to his wife's body; her breasts will be used to
feed the child and her attention, even in pregnancy, is no longer
exclusively on her spouse as once it might have been, or as he
believes that it should be.

The most extreme form of domestic violence is homicide. The
New Zealand police said they could not provide us with detailed
statistical information of how many deaths were domestic in nature.
We wonder why this information is not available. The *New Zealand
Herald* (14 January, 1989) supplied an analysis of the thirty-nine
homicides that had occurred in the upper North Island during 1988.
About a half of these deaths appeared to be domestic in nature, – a
figure confirmed by Alison Gray in a paper prepared for the Family
Violence Research Project (87). We know from overseas research
(76) that a quarter of all homicides in the United States occur in

domestic situations and involve people in a relationship. Broadly speaking, men are more likely to kill in the bedroom, and women in the kitchen; men kill for sexual motives, women in extremity or self-defence. This raises a question which we have not yet addressed, namely, that of sexual jealousy. While this is the stuff of Greek tragedies, airport novels, and television soap operas, it is also the stuff of everyday life. The men concerned regard women as their sexual property, and any other consorts, real or imagined, the women might have as sexual thieves and predators. Violence attributed to a sexual motive can often more accurately be ascribed to outraged dependency. Over-mothered men expect domestic services more appropriate to slaves than to spouses. There are many men who have never looked after themselves and do not know how to do so. They expect that their wives will not only do everything that their mothers used to do, but sleep with them as well! Some also expect their wife to contribute equally to the family income, yet when they do so may feel usurped as the breadwinner. Sexual jealousy therefore may be better regarded as just part of a more complex motivation for violence.

Men, as well as women, are supposed to play Happy Families and will blame their partner when things go wrong. As a number of commentators point out (76, 77, 83), it is not sexuality but the structure of relationships in a family prone to violence that leads to domestic homicide. And the same may be true of many situations where infidelity becomes the trigger that releases violent behaviour. All human behaviour is motivated by a complex web of antecedents. The judicial preoccupation with motive leads to over-simplifications and attribution to single causes. Crimes of passions are also power crimes, crimes involving threats to status, security or self-esteem, ambivalence over dependency, with maybe a dash of envy, greed, avarice, sloth, anger, and the other deadly sins thrown in.

One reason why domestic violence is likely to be more frequent than violence outside the family is because there is less risk of serious repercussions. If you strike your boss, you will probably lose your job and be charged with assault, but if you strike your wife, she may do nothing (except perhaps leave you). As Goode points out, because husbands are bigger, have higher status and earn more money they are 'top dog' within the family. Women and children have most to lose if they reject or react to domestic violence. They may have no place to run, no financial or other resources by which they can survive alone, or seek retribution from their attackers (183).

Because the home is private, its secrets are controlled by whoever is most powerful within it. Furthermore, police, prosecutors, courts, and other agents of the state are biased towards the preservation and perpetuation of the family and are supported in this by vociferous lobbies with unrealistic views of what families should be.

Thus domestic violence imprisons the victim rather than the criminal, a situation which has in the past been tacitly condoned by the state since to intervene would involve real financial costs as well as increase the load on social services. Until 1987, police practice in cases of domestic violence was to play a very low-key role. Unless the woman was prepared to press charges, the violent male was not routinely arrested. A pilot research programme directed towards reform was carried out in 1986 by Greg Ford in Hamilton (65). A new policy was adopted. An arrest was made wherever there was evidence of assault. Procedures were initiated actively to link the victim with support services. This action research was an outstanding success. In 80 per cent of cases, the violence stopped after the arrest. Clearly, police felt happier, too, with their more active and decisive role, since the project led to a national review of policy, endorsed and applied in 1987. Although not all police, particularly older officers, have been able to change their attitudes, Ford notes that about 2,000 extra arrests are now made annually for domestic violence. Arrest may be a crude tool with no guarantee of correction or protection. But it is a decisive intervention that may initiate changes in what were previously intractable and damaging relationships.

Perpetrators of domestic violence may be handled by a policy, available for first offenders, known as diversion. After an initial court appearance, the offender may be directed to attend a course in anger management conducted by groups such as Men for Non-Violence. Here, males learn how to handle their anger in non-violent ways by recognising their body signs and by making use of time-out, that is, taking themselves out of the potentially violent situation. If the course is completed satisfactorily, charges are dropped.

Those who have never been in a situation of domestic violence may find it difficult to understand why women, particularly, put up with it. Why don't they just leave? There are always many reasons – fear, threats, children, dependency – but three reasons dominate.

Firstly, in many families violence has come to be accepted as normal, something that must be endured either 'for the sake of the children' or because of the background of violence within which the parents themselves grew up. Secondly, because the victim often gets blamed, there is great shame attached to publicly acknowledging domestic violence (as is also the case with incest and rape within marriage). Sometimes the husband's aggression is followed by guilt and remorse which may be mistaken for love; if this leads to a linkage between beating and sexual intercourse the cycle may become compulsive. Violent men may collapse into a blubbering heap of dependency if their wife-mother threatens to leave – and who will look after the children? Thirdly, there is often no place to go, particularly if the woman's own family was as bad or worse, and if financial resources are limited or non-existent. But above all else is the motive of sheer, and justified, terror. Fear paralyses the victim's whole condition, preoccupies her everyday thought. She fears to stay; she fears to go. The threats of reprisal, whether overt or implied, are real.

Women's refuges are one way to protect women from immediate threat of further violence. The first refuge was established in Christchurch in 1973, followed by one in Auckland in 1975, and one in Dunedin in 1976. By 1981 there were seventeen refuges nationwide, and by 1987 there were forty-eight refuges affiliated to the National Collective of Independent Women's Refuges. More than 3,000 women and 5,000 children were cared for in refuges during 1989. Refuges for Maori women now provide shelter in Auckland, Hamilton, Wellington, Christchurch, and Palmerston North, though all refuges are now working to meet more effectively the needs of the various cultural groups who come to them for help. The demand is increasing (3,200 women were cared for in 1989, compared with 3,065 in 1988), but there is still no national policy concerning the way refuges fit into the framework of rehabilitation and prevention. They need to be seen as more than just emergency shelters (164).

The basic problem that must be dealt with in domestic violence is the immature, dependent, but domineering male. He is not always big, nor flamboyantly macho in style; indeed, he is more likely to be rather pathetic and socially inadequate, comfortable only in the superficial mateship of his own gender, or an isolate who has grown up believing that it is acceptable to beat those you are supposed to love.

McMaster and Swain (134) rightly regard what they call the 'ideology of men', beliefs based on male strength, dominance and power, and conversely, female weakness and inferiority, as the fundamental background to domestic attacks.

A society, or institutions within it such as the police or welfare services, must do what can be done once incidents occur or violent relationships emerge from the mask of domestic privacy. But behind incidences, practices, and provisions lie patterns. The pattern of the permission some men give themselves freely to express their violent feelings in hurtful actions against others is part of the ideology of maleness that must begin to change.

We will discuss the reduction of violence later, but the peculiar nature of domestic assault requires some special comment now. We will not see change in this area until there are radical changes in fundamental social concepts which have been enshrined in social practice and in law. The family should not be so inviolate or so private that it is to be preserved whatever the costs to individuals within it. The state and its agencies have the capacity to be better parents than many who are presently parents (even if in the past the state has been a truly neglectful parent to many).

The sexist character of our society must be changed, and along with it all those social agencies that glorify violence and thus legitimise it. For example, the connection between pornography and the debasement and sexual abuse of women is intimately involved in this, as is the ideology that attempts to justify rape. We must realise that domestic violence produces enormous hidden costs which are no longer acceptable. If human suffering is not enough to justify active social programmes, then we should calculate the financial costs to society overall. Social economists have put figures on alcohol use (180), the cost of tobacco addiction (248), traffic accidents (152), and many other social pathologies (see Chapter 10), but we know of no similar exercise to express the extent of the costs we all pay because some of us are uncontrollably violent at home.

New Zealand law has recently recognised that rape can occur within marriage, whether legal or de facto. We shall use the term marital rape to refer to any act of forced sexual access in any established relationship, not just in legal marriage. Forced sex is common both as a cause and a consequence of wife battering. There are no New Zealand incidence studies, but American figures suggest that sexual assaults by husbands on their wives occur at least twice as often as other rape (62). Marital rape is the most frequent kind of rape, according to Russell (212). Incidence figures from women's refuge shelters (78, 170, 229) reveal that a third of the women seeking refuge from battering husbands also suffer from marital rape. Russell reported that 14 per cent of nearly 1,000 women included in her random and representative survey of women in heterosexual partnerships in San Francisco described sexual encounters where force was used or where the woman was helpless and therefore unable to give consent (212).

The literature, largely American, emphasises not only the severe mental trauma that accompanies such incidents but also the continuing effects on all later sexual experiences, whether forced or not, and whether with the same partner or with others. Marital rape totally erodes the ability of the victim to maintain or renew trust in the relationship. The woman raped by a stranger at least does not have to wake every morning and see the man who raped her. Marital rape is a particularly debasing and humiliating act, and it is not surprising that it so often involves coercion into anal intercourse and sado-masochistic practices.

For all its horror, marital rape is simply one violent practice in marriages where violence is endemic. It never occurs without other forms of violence, but is especially humiliating and destructive of the victim's self-esteem because it leaves no visible wounds and cannot easily be openly acknowledged or freely discussed. To be coerced into conspiracy over one's own exploitation induces a paralysis of will. For these reasons, while there has been legal recognition of the crime, the new law is unlikely to reduce the incidence of marital rape nor is it likely to lead to prosecution and convictions. If we are to do something about marital rape, we must change the sexist and violent nature of our society. We will discuss rape further in the next chapter, when we examine violence by strangers.

Another shadowy area in the family is the violence that exists between siblings who may have as many reasons to hate as to love one another. Other members of the family as well as outsiders are likely to condone this as just something that happens in childhood. Well, that may be so, but it happens more in the childhood of some than of others, and it is probably the most frequent form of violence, overall (239). Not only do children within families establish their own pecking order but they frequently use and encourage their friends to victimise their siblings. In violent families there may be little attempt by parents to curb sibling abuse. The exploited and oppressed frequently find someone on whom they can act out their anger and resentment. Siblings may be the most convenient target.

There is virtually no New Zealand research on this matter to date, so let us turn, briefly, to some from the United States. In a national study, more than half of the children acknowledged having made an attack on a sibling during the year prior to the study, and over a third had committed a severe assault. These were not just childish pranks; they persisted even in the 15–17 age group, and included beatings, murders by smothering, by gunshot, with knives and other lethal objects. Many incidents look suspiciously like copy-cat crimes based on television scenarios. Consistent with most other forms of violence, more boys were involved than girls, and more severely involved than girls. The authors expressed some shock at the extent of the sibling abuse revealed by their survey, but went on to say that perhaps their surprise was simply because no one had gathered such data before (239). That leads us to ask why not? One possible answer is that, as with smacking children, we think of sibling abuse as normal unless there is some weird aspect to it like incest or torture.

In the absence of local data, we simply ask the reader to pause, to reflect on his or her own childhood, and remember. Were there violent incidents between siblings either in your own family or in other families in your neighbourhood? Did you ever hit a sibling? Were you ever hit, terrorised or abused by one? Sibling violence is the domestic side of the violence that occurs everywhere between children as they seek power over one another, act out the models that they see at home, on television, or elsewhere around them. Why should we be surprised when childhood reflects the violence that is part of the world of adult behaviour and the cultural patterns that permit its expression?

Those patterns are also projected in the violence parents perpetrate upon children. We allow parents to hit children. Were that not so, a great deal of physical abuse would never occur. But the *causes* of child abuse are legion. We will focus not upon them but upon prevention and protection.

The protection of children from parental abuse has a patchy history in this country because it violates our notions of the sanctity of parental rights. The great nineteenth-century reformers brought about changes in the status of children through laws concerning social welfare, employment, and education. Almost a century later the focus on infant health produced a further set of provisions, but one area of childhood remained almost totally unprotected. During the vital preschool years the care of children is almost totally left to the wisdom of parents within the home. These are the years in which considerable violence towards children occurs. The previous neglect of child protection has been somewhat reduced in the recent Children, Young Persons and their Families Act. Even in this legislative revision which broadens the definition of family to include the whanau or extended family the state remains reluctant to interfere in parental rights or to infringe in any way on the traditional sanctity of the family. Subsequently, many children still suffer at the hands of their parents.

Even the state itself acknowledges that it has been a poor parent. Many of the most violent members of our society have been wards of the state and have suffered institutional neglect and violence. But violent offenders can also be traced to families where bad parenting has hurt them to such an extent that they will spend the rest of their lives seeking revenge on society.

Children have been hurt and maimed by their parents through the ages (47). When Henry Kempe and his associates gave child abuse its modern definition in 1962 (109) the New Zealand reaction followed the pattern which Kempe himself later described (110). At first, in the denial phase, there was little recognition that physical and sexual abuse were any kind of problem in a society which prided itself on being 'a great place to bring up kids'. Although cases undeniably occurred, they were thought to be so outrageous and rare that they could only have been committed by psychopaths. As we moved through the next stage, that of public awareness, the press increasingly probed the subject, often with lurid accounts, and alerted the paediatric and child-care professions to look for signs of physical abuse. At this point, we might have expected a commission of inquiry, but, better still, we got a full-blown national research study (59). Consequently, we moved fairly quickly through to Kempe's third stage, the beginnings of public provision for the physically abused, and rapidly on to the fourth, the recognition of emotional abuse. In the last few years we have reached the fifth stage, the recognition of the extent and severity of sexual abuse.

No one could claim that we have yet reached stage six, where all children have the kind of care and protection that they need for full emotional, physical, intellectual, and social development; we still have a long way to go.

In spite of the fact that a national committee for the prevention of child abuse was established in 1980, we still do not have reliable incidence figures nor anything like an adequate prevention or therapy service (73). In a country as small as New Zealand these should not have been difficult to incorporate into the various health and welfare screenings which occur. But resistance is strong. There is great reluctance to break families. There are territorial disputes involving incompatible goals and operating methods between various professions (general practitioners, social workers, police, lawyers, teachers, child protection volunteers). Child protection will cost – who will pay?

The currently accepted figure for the incidence of child abuse from the national study (3 per 10,000 children) is far too low to be credible. Given the levels of other forms of violence throughout our society, something very strange would have to be happening for the incidence of child abuse to be this low.

Since 1980 there has been a clear agenda for the establishment of child protection procedures, as well as for preventative methods to which we shall refer shortly (73). Why has progress on this agenda been so painfully slow?

The answers are political. Children are, themselves, powerless; they carry no votes and so their advocates have little status. The information base concerning their condition is pitifully thin and scrappy compared with, say knowledge of how to grow grass, or breed dairy cows, or prevent heart attacks. There is a tiny but vociferous pressure group defending 'traditional' family values which wishes to impose its moral and ethical standards on everyone else and which, for the better part of the last decade, has wielded more parliamentary influence than its numbers or its ideology have warranted. There is also the matter of cost. Many needed reforms, such as effective child protection teams and in-service training courses for professionals of all kinds, cost money.

General practitioners, and the medical profession generally, have been less than helpful and have been partly responsible for preventing the introduction of mandatory reporting of child abuse. Other established child-care professions have also backed away from their clear public duty. The government has not yet ratified the United Nations Declaration on the Rights of the Child. The recent appointment of a children's commissioner through the Children, Young Persons and their Families Act is a first step, but it is too early to tell how effective the role will be.

Intervention programmes are costly too. Monaghan and her associates in Dunedin clearly demonstrated the value of screening all mothers who passed through their obstetric unit to determine the risk to the child of abuse (154). This research shows that screening is quite practicable and could be nationally implemented immediately if there was the will, and the money, to do so. If accident and emergency units at each major hospital were staffed with professionals alert to the signs of child abuse (which are well known), we would be dealing with one area where problems frequently surface. Too often the professionals don't recognise the signs or, if they do, regard it as someone else's concern. They may not be trained  or resourced to handle such matters. Even when systems are put in place, such as registers of previous or known abusers, they often go unused.

In recent research, Joy Hay gave training in child abuse detection to a sample of teachers (93). Her criterion tests showed that teachers often fail to identify child abuse and are hesitant in taking action through existing agencies. As has often been found, passive training, by means of literature alone, achieved very little. The training programme increased the teachers' knowledge of indicators and of help available, and their acceptance of responsibility. Awareness and identification of abuse increased dramatically and reporting of suspected cases also increased. Such research demonstrates the strategic importance of the classroom as another point at which child abuse screening can occur.

We believe that if obstetric units, Plunket and public health nurses, general practitioners, and school teachers were all equipped to do this job, we would have a service in place which would tell us how many children are at risk and what these risks are, and alert us to the necessary steps which should be taken. However, if such a service were operating efficiently nation-wide, there would be such a landslide of demand for existing child-care services that they would never cope. This is not, of course, an argument in favour of doing nothing. The nettle should be grasped. We advocate mandatory reporting by all these groups. Systems can be made to cope. The Children, Young Persons and their Families Act, which came into force late in 1989, abandoned mandatory reporting and child protection teams in favour of an enhanced role for family involvement in decision making about the care of the child. This was done in the interests of cultural sensitivity, but another reason might have been the lack of resources to cope with a possible flood of reported cases.

What can be done to prevent child abuse? Physical punishment of children must simply be outlawed. As we stated in *Spare the Rod* the risks to children are too great for it to be allowed to continue. We endorse training for parenthood. We think that the literature on child abuse is now sufficiently developed and explicit for it to be included in parent training programmes wherever they occur. It should not be glossed over. We should not be saying to prospective parents at an antenatal class, 'none of you is going to be the kind of parent who abuses your child'. Every potential parent needs to confront the possibility that some day, somewhere, the temptation and the pressure to act abusively may occur; and if not to them, then maybe to their partner, or in their wider family, or neighbourhood. We all have responsibility, whether or not the state enacts mandatory reporting. The unthinkable must be thought about, and instruction given on how to recognise the possibility of avoiding it.

Sexual abuse is the result of a disastrous conjunction of attitudes towards sex, towards family privacy, the permission some men give themselves, power in private domains, poor protection of children's rights and the place of women in our society.

The first published New Zealand research on child sexual abuse was by Miriam Saphira based on 315 self-report returns from a *New Zealand Woman's Weekly* questionnaire (219). This research revealed an astonishing amount of intrafamilial sexual abuse, much of it incestuous, and predominantly of girls under the age of eleven. Intrafamilial abuse tends to persist over long periods of time and has quite a different history and progress from the predatory activities of habitual but roving child molesters. The respondents to Saphira's survey were a self-selected group, and her survey could therefore give no sure indication of just how frequently child sexual abuse occurred.

The general literature on sexual abuse indicates that it very frequently goes unreported, that required criteria for proof result in a low conviction rate and that there is great reluctance to face up to the extensive, long term trauma the victims suffer (177). After centuries of concealment of such acts, virtually of the acceptance of incest and denial of its consequences, slowly, our society has begun to face the realities. But still the research is thin on the ground, of low impact and greeted more with defensiveness and denial than with recognition that there is a substantial problem to be faced – by everyone, not just by the victims.

An often quoted study, conducted by Wellington Rape Crisis, asked secondary pupils if they had ever been touched in a sexual way when they did not want to be. A third of the girls replied that they had and this figure has become the source of the often stated claim that one in three girls is sexually abused before reaching the age of eighteen. One needs to note the potentially very broad definition of 'touched in sexual way' and remember that the person doing the touching was not limited to a parent or even an adult male relative (63).

In 1988 researchers at the Otago Medical School found that 10 per cent of their sample reported that they had experienced sexual abuse involving genital contact. In half of the cases, the perpetrator was a stranger and in 39 per cent he was a relative. Of these, stepfathers (10 per cent) were the most frequent, followed by grandfathers (7 per cent) and fathers and brothers (each 5 per cent) and a few odd uncles and others (161).

Jane von Dadelszen studied the frequency of sexual abuse among girls in the care of the Department of Social Welfare. Two-thirds of them had experienced sexual abuse, half of them more than once. Only a tenth of the abusers were strangers, about a half were family members and a fifth were friends or acquaintances of the girl (253). In an Auckland study only 15 per cent of the children were sexually abused by a stranger (84).

Gillian Pow provides a useful literature review of the short- and long-term consequences of sexual abuse (177). Lack of trust, guilt, and shame are common reactions and difficulty in establishing satisfactory sexual relationships in adulthood is often reported. The Otago study found that women who had been sexually assaulted in childhood were significantly more likely than women who had not, to suffer from depressive or anxiety disorders. Women who had been assaulted in adulthood were even more likely to suffer from a psychiatric disorder (161). Recent reports link sexual abuse with eating disorders such as anorexia and bulimia (228).

Finkelhor reported that one-fifth of a college sample survey of American women reported sexual victimisation during childhood; half of this was intrafamilial (61). Other estimates of incidence in the United States (247) vary so widely that there can be no real confidence in any of them. However the conclusions everywhere are the same: child sexual victimisation is much more prevalent than was once believed: it is mostly females who are assaulted; and it is mostly from within the family – from relatives or the mother's male consort(s) or brothers' male mates – that the assault comes.

Here in New Zealand the National Advisory Committee on the Prevention of Child Abuse published *Guidelines for the Investigation and Management of the Sexual Abuse of Children* in 1986. There are two broad categories: intrafamilial sexual molestation, and molestation by more distant relatives and violators outside the family. The problems of detection and reporting and the special sensitivities needed are fully covered in the *Guidelines*. The horror and outrage everyone feels about child sexual abuse has led to these guidelines being tighter, tougher and more mandatory than those for physical abuse (162).

The urge that leads to the secret, seductive terrorist behaviour of the incest perpetrator may be very different from that of the attack child molester. But there are common elements. A sexually inadequate person, usually male, *takes,* by assumed right and by coercion whether seductive or forceful or by deceit from a powerless victim, something he believes that he cannot get otherwise. He can dominate no other this way. He rejects the rules. He seeks out vulnerable victims (14).

In every case there is a history behind why *this* person committed *this* act. But also, to do it the victim must be de-personalised, the trance-like theatre of violent enactment entered, a psychological state induced in victim and violator and reality itself be raped.

Somehow men who sexually abuse children must be made to accept that such conduct is totally intolerable. Much effort is currently being put into warning girls of the dangers of sexual abuse, but this puts the onus upon the female victim. The men who perpetrate such assaults may have failed to learn that they are morally wrong, but more often they know but do not care. They have come from families which did not instil such prohibitions, but how did they not learn from general society, how prohibited such acts are? They may have passed through schools where it was never confronted as an issue. We must use every means to ensure that every male does get the message and school is where that message must be taught, frankly, openly, unstintingly, since everyone goes there. But it is not enough to simply insist that 'thou shalt not'. We believe that there must be full examination of the cultural roots of violence; everyone must understand.

Contrary to popular belief and the publicity given to exceptional cases, reoffending rates for people convicted of sex offences are low. Rape and attempted rape offenders have a low probability of reconviction; child molesters and exhibitionists are more likely to reoffend than rapists or incest offenders. A new facility for sex offenders was opened at Rolleston prison in Christchurch in 1989, with the aim of providing counselling and training in an environment more like the outside world than a prison. Department of Justice figures in 1989 showed that less than 10 per cent of child molesters, and only two out of the eighty men released after serving a term of imprisonment for incest in the previous three years had reoffended. However, the public outcry when reoffending occurs has clearly motivated the government to provide this special facility, even though its response to the recommendations of the Ministerial Committee of Enquiry into Prisons in 1989 (151) (which include habilitation centres for those much more likely to reoffend) has been decidedly lukewarm.

We can take considerable comfort from the professionals working with single incident and incest sex offenders who claim that re-education is worth the effort (14). We can also learn from them much that will be useful in preventative strategies.

All the coercive sexual violations, rape, child molestation, flashing, voyeurism, pornographic addiction, incest, and forced indecent acts are obsessional behaviours. Their origins are varied but frequently lie in the perpetrators' own earlier seduction and resulting guilt and gender confusions. Patterns of repetitive satisfaction are constructed. Available cultural justifications such as the doctrine of irresistible impulse or animal nature, maintain the behaviour. They form compulsive cycles of the kind Karen Horney explained as a basis for therapy over forty years ago (97).

Obsessional compulsive sex offending can be corrected as the work of William Marshall, the Canadian consultant to the Rolleston Kia Marama project has shown (15). But this is intensive and demanding therapeutic work; very costly in human terms. Earlier we said that education is one key; therapeutic re-education is another.

In 1986 the Minister of Social Welfare, the Honourable Ann Hercus, established the Family Violence Prevention Co-ordinating Committee, a body made up of government and other agencies. These include the Departments of Education, Health, Maori Affairs, Women's Affairs, Justice, Police, Pacific Island Affairs, Family Courts, the Accident Compensation Corporation, and community agencies dealing with aspects of violence such as the National Collective of Independent Women's Refuges, the National Collective of Rape Crisis and Related Groups, Men for Non-Violence, the Pacific Island Women's Project and Network, and Te Kakano o te Whanau. The committee's aim is to co-ordinate the activities of the various agencies in terms of both support and prevention to ensure that all programmes operate in a culturally appropriate manner.

The most visible activity of this committee has been a television campaign featuring an ex-All Black who told violent men it is not manly to be violent, and a former television personality who emerged from a large group of singing women with a message of support for beaten women. In addition, it has commissioned research, published a newsletter, issued an information booklet listing various social services and helping groups, and acted as an information exchange point and resource centre. To date, there is no way of assessing its effectiveness in actually reducing family violence, but there can be no doubt that its publicity has played a role in raising the level of public awareness of the problem.

Such awareness is essential. A society which fails to protect its children and young women from violence and sexual abuse can bear little claim to be civilised or decent.

As a society we may be on the way towards a healthier, safer domestic scene. Young people are learning to be franker, more assertive, more aware. The servicing of problems as they arise still needs to be swifter, surer, less bureaucratic, better and more constantly funded. More and more voluntary and community-based services are available. We are moving from awareness to action, but progress is glacially slow and the energy easily dispersed.

We know at least some of the things that need to be done. Around the country women's groups, victim groups, men's anger management groups, prison groups, peace groups, Maori groups and probably dozens of others as well have begun to programme ways out. Slowly these efforts are forming networks, supporting one another. When and if they can all engage in a concerted critique of our society, we could be more confident that the dark ages are truly behind us and not just ahead.

# 5

# Violence Away

Statistically, New Zealanders display very much the same range of violent activities as any other Western industrial society. Homicide, assault, rape, vandalism, arson, and other offences against the person and against property are found everywhere. Such acts are seen by the public as a rising tide of lawlessness remorselessly pressing against the thin barricades of law and order and the agencies of control. Is this an appropriate perception?

All of this gets due, and sometimes undue, attention in the media and contributes to a sort of on-going industry. At each election, the law and order issue is hauled out, dusted off and hawked around the countryside, usually resulting in a promise of action. The action which follows usually consists of a committee or commission whose reports in future will doubtless be greatly facilitated by the recycling of previous reports through the word processor. Between elections, governments tinker with penalties and the definition of offences, manipulate the numbers in the police force and respond to the eruption of public outrage that often follows a particularly dramatic criminal incident. Why some such incidents are responded to in this way and others are ignored has a lot to do with the time of the year, the marginality of the government's majority, and who happens to be pushing the bandwagon. But whenever and why it starts to move, its passage and progress are fairly predictable. Violence in our society is not random, it is patterned. And so, too, are our reactions to it.

The Department of Justice submission to the Committee of Inquiry into violence in 1986 included information on all the murders committed between 1950 and 1985 (49). While the number of murders fluctuates from year to year (there were twenty-five in 1981 but only seven in 1982), there has been a steady increase over the years. The average number of murders between 1960 and 1964 was six. For the five-year period twenty years later (1980–4), this had risen to twenty-seven. The annual figure starts to rise after 1975. Other violent offences have also risen steadily. In 1985 there were eleven times as many violent offences as in 1960.

Six per cent of the 202 murderers were female and 94 per cent male. This ratio did not change over the period of the study. Sixty-one per cent of the murderers had previous criminal records, but the proportion of murderers who have histories of violent offending has increased in recent years. Of those who committed murder between 1960 and 1969, 23 per cent had convictions for violent offending, compared with nearly half (48 per cent) of those who committed murder between 1980 and 1985.

The educational level of murderers changed little over the period of the study. Only 10 per cent of murderers in the 1980s had managed to progress beyond the third form, compared to 4 per cent in the period between 1960 and 1969. The average age of murderers has changed little over the decades, remaining at about twenty-nine; the murderers in the study ranged in age from fourteen to sixty-eight.

Another feature that has remained constant has been the proportion of victims known to their murderers – about three-quarters. Nearly a third of the victims were family members. So far this report has revealed an extraordinary sociological predictability in the background of murderers.

Two factors have changed markedly over the years. One is the proportion of unemployed who feature in the homicide statistics. Until about 1970, only 16 per cent of the murderers were out of work at the time of the murder but the percentage has risen to 55 per cent in the 1980s. Of course over this decade unemployment increased dramatically in the total population, so the change is in employment, not in the nature of murder or murderers. The second change relates to the number of murderers who were Maori. In the first two decades of the study (1950-69), 23 per cent of committed murderers were Maori, a figure which rose in the 1970s to 25 per cent and in the 1980s to 48 per cent. The label 'Maori' may be meaningless in this context, since we know nothing of how culturally Maori these offenders are. Before anything can be concluded from these statistics they need to be placed in the context of general social trends such as unemployment, migration, and family breakdown.

In all this statistical information, it is difficult to see anything unique about New Zealand homicides and assaults. They have

*Violence in New Zealand*

increased in proportion to economic hardship and social deprivation. The government and the public at large find it convenient to focus attention upon the crime rates and the criminals because the social and economic problems which lie behind them are so difficult to resolve. Yet by world standards, New Zealand cities and streets, homes, and parks are safe places, even though they have become less so in the last decade (7). And our homicide rate of 2.2 per 100,000 of population is similar to that of England (2.24), lower than that of Australia (2.73), and much, much lower than that of the USA (9.60) (119).

Much of the increase in violent offending is associated with crimes against property. Property crime is almost everywhere committed by the deprived against the privileged. Theft, burglary, and robbery are crimes of gain. Vandalism and arson are crimes of destruction. Car theft may have a range of motive reason: joy-riding, lack of transport, bravado, sale or plunder, or simply the desire to wreck. If killing occurs in association with these property crimes the context is very different from that of intentional homicide.

However, crime statistics must be interpreted with caution. The use of percentages in isolation can imply an exaggerated increase in low frequency crimes. Different ways of defining crimes or gathering statistics, and differences in policing methods can affect reported crime rates.

Newspaper headlines can contribute to public alarm. 'Soaring Violence in Crime Concerns' (*Waikato Times*, 25 August 1989) headlines an article which records that although current crime had risen nationally by 7.5 per cent, homicides had dropped by the same amount and seven districts had actually reported drops in crime overall. Nevertheless, any increase in crime, however small, provides an opportunity for a Police Association spokesperson to lament the lack of police resources, and for Opposition politicians to berate the government of the day for being 'soft' on crime.

Rape has received a great deal of attention from the public and from both political parties. Rape is the only crime where the victim is often as much on trial as the accused and in which, because it is unlikely that there will be independent witnesses, the prosecution will have difficulty in securing a conviction. In 1981 there were sixty-four rape convictions; this had risen to seventy-nine in 1985. However, in 1984 there were 381 complaints of rape, of which the police decided to prosecute fewer than a third (29 per cent). Of the 111 cases prosecuted, a conviction was obtained in eighty cases (72 per cent), although this means that only 21 per cent of the rapes initially reported to the police resulted in a conviction (224). Criminologist Warren Young has estimated that only 4 per cent of rapes ever result in a prosecution (259). Is it any wonder that victims of rape who initiate and then suffer the ordeal of police and court procedures often ask themselves if it was worth it?

A major symposium on rape was held in 1981 (143) and a two-volume study was issued in 1983 by the Department of Justice (48). There are a number of issues which lie behind this attention. There are serious problems within the criminal justice system in dealing with evidence, the difficulty of conviction, and the feminist view that the justice system, in this area, is far from just. Attitudes to sexuality have become more liberal, which may also have led some men to believe they have a greater right of sexual access to women. Society has become suddenly more liberal in respect of pornography, and the depiction of male sexual violence has become quite fashionable, even in G-rated movies, videos and TV 'soaps'.

There has been a cost involved in 'taking the wraps off' rape. When it was a taboo subject, there was less inducement to copy-cat crime. Rape has become almost a badge of membership in some groups in our society.

Rape is denied by both men and women. Some men still think, 'I bet she asked for it' or 'she probably deserved it'. Others distance themselves from the perpetrator by claiming that no 'decent' man would ever do such a thing. There are women, too, who say, 'she must have asked for it, walking at night like that. I don't walk at night alone therefore it won't happen to me'. The attitude that 'only sluts get raped' still prevails.

Of all the violent crimes, rape has generated the most myths in popular folklore (33, 224). Contrary to public belief, most rapes are not committed on the streets at night by a stranger but at the home of either the victim or the rapist by someone who is very often known to the victim (39). Women do not get raped because they flaunt their sexuality: victims can be any female – from little girls to very old women. Rapists are not always either young men in the full flush of sexual desire or 'dirty old men'. They too cover the whole age range.

While less recent literature (4) suggests that anger and hostility towards the woman victim, rather than sexual lust, is an important motivation, modern perspectives regard rape as an act of power, of domination (224). Most rapists are not sexually deprived but are either in regular sexual relationships or have licit sex available to them if they seek it. The purchase of sex on the streets is available to all men. But that is not what the rapist is after. There is also the myth that rapists are sexually inadequate but this, too, is not the case. The sexually inadequate peep or flash or seek out children (14).

These myths are carried in the collective consciousness of our society. They are perpetrated through literature, movies, and videos.

Especially pernicious is the scenario where the woman resists sexual advances, is raped, and enjoys the sexual encounter (54, 189). This is a frequent theme in pornographic videos but in milder form it pervades the popular media. Even when the censor cuts a scene, it just leaves a gap where the rape ought to be. Men who watch this kind of material internalise the message that women really want sex and enjoy being raped, even though they may initially say no. Such messages give men permission to rape. Implicit rape scenes give vunerable men as much (or more) permission as overt depiction. The message that women wish to be violated to fulfil their sexual desires must be banished for ever from popular culture.

Some minor changes to the law and improvement in judicial practice have lessened the ordeal of the victim. Rape crisis centres provide support for both recent victims, and those who were raped in the past and who have long carried a secret burden. Victim impact assessment is now routine so that the court will have adequate evaluation of the damage which has occurred.

A substantial study of rape victims was included in the Department of Justice's Rape Study in 1983. In the first volume, Warren Young discussed the law, court, and judicial proceedings relating to rape (259). While much can be done to protect the victim from the distressing experience of legal proceedings, the basic problem is the reluctance of victims to report at all. Young believed that changes in the law and practice would encourage a higher level of reporting, but he acknowledged that rape puts the victim in such an invidious social position that legal changes are unlikely to have much effect. Rather, he put his trust in community education and the establishment of comprehensive, readily available, and adequate victim support services.

The victim must be given every protection from public exposure, yet the public must be informed when rape has occurred, and by whom. It is almost impossible to punish the perpetrator without further punishing the victim. The characteristics of rapists are so diverse that it is likewise almost impossible to run educational and publicity campaigns which do not deepen women's mistrust of men in general. It is regrettable that half of the population must distrust the other.half because of the actions of a few. This seems unfair, and many worthy men may feel grossly offended. It is ironic that it is the non-rapist who must establish his credentials. But all men are capable of rape, and those who reject that possibility are simply distancing themselves from a major social problem caused by their own gender. This is not a cause which women must fight alone.

The second volume of the Department of Justice's report consisted of research studies. The first described an in-depth interview study of fifty women rape victims, four of whom had been raped twice (236). The sample was small and adventitious rather than systematic, and was used by the authors largely to illustrate various topics and themes, such as why some women report rape and some women do not, the circumstances under which rape occurs, the experiences which victims report of police procedures, and the court process. These fifty women also commented on the sources and quality of support or help that they received. There is a special section on rape within marriage.

The recommendations from this study (and there were a great many) were wide ranging. This is understandable, because the area of rape, as social policy, is deeply perplexing. The injury inflicted not only by the attack but also by subsequent legal proceedings (if the rape is reported at all) persists in memory and may deepen rather than be resolved by time. Because of this, we will never know how many rapists go uncaught and unchallenged, or how much damage they do to their victims.

The recommendations in the study emphasise that the existence of rape must be frankly acknowledged and publicly discussed. They urge that the police employ women officers and that only they should deal with the victim and in circumstances that are more sensitive to the special nature of sexual assault. They call for judicial proceedings to be reoriented and restructured to take account of the victim's special needs, and for support services to be universally available and publicly funded.

The Justice Department Rape Study also contained a report on rape complaints which revealed that most rape complainants know the name of the rapist (231). Even in gang rapes (one in five of all complaints) at least one member of the gang was known to the victim. Contrary to popular belief, rapists do not often inflict serious physical injury on the victim, but usually use force such as grabbing and pushing and threats of physical injury or injury to the woman's reputation.

The information in this report is distressingly familiar. From the police records, there would appear to be two kinds of rape. In one, the victim is likely to be young, unemployed, and attacked in a public place by a stranger or someone she knows by name but only casually. The other, more frequent rape is by someone acquainted with the victim. The former feature more frequently in the police records while the latter, overwhelmingly, predominate in the records of rape crisis centres and support groups, which show that rape victims cover a wide range of ages and are most likely to be raped in their own home by someone they know.

The complaint data show that the majority of defendants (64 per cent) plead guilty. In the year of the study, there were twenty-seven rape defendants who proceeded to a jury trial; of these, thirteen were convicted of rape or attempted rape. The defence usually turns on one of two issues: the allegation that consent was given and therefore there was no rape, or that the accused was misidentified (231).

The police, it seems, loathe the whole business. They generally despise the rapists and have an embarrassed but quite genuine desire to lessen the unpleasant nature of the experience for the complainant. The frequent absence of any corroborative evidence makes this and child sexual abuse peculiar issues in terms of court procedures.

These studies preceded the general legislative review of 1986 when the definition of rape was changed to that of sexual violation, a husband's exemption from the charge of rape was withdrawn, and a woman's past sexual history could be referred to only with the explicit permission of the presiding judge. Strengthening the role of rape crisis centres and women's refuges is clearly part of government intention, but so far funding is still very limited.

Anti-rape education remains still at the discretion of schools. Despite the worthy efforts of voluntary groups, we are still a long way from rearing a generation of men for whom rape is an unthinkable act. And for all progress that we make, there is an unknown degree of counteraction caused by the depiction of rape, near rape, or what might have been rape, in videos, movies, and television.

In their submission to the Roper Committee of Inquiry into Violence the police collected information on 100 prisoners convicted of rape and found a high correlation between rape and general offending (150). These 100 may be the worst the police could find; their rate of offending was an appalling average of 24.7 convictions each. Forty-three of this group were Pakeha, fifty-seven were Polynesian, and twenty-six belonged to gangs most of which were Maori. Gang members committed an average of 30.7 offences each. The police conclude that greater police pressure will have to be placed on gang members, even though such pressure will almost certainly increase offending. While much attention is given to the more lurid incidents of gang rape, indecent assaults and individual rapes by gang members, it is necessary to keep the issue of gang membership in perspective. Total gang membership throughout the country is around 4,000, a rise from just over 2,000 in 1986.

The aim of gangs is not to wage war on society, even though one might well gain that impression from the media. The major purpose of gangs is to provide affiliation and support for their members. They are a substitute for family for individuals whose own families are unsatisfactory, unsupportive, or simply non-existent. Many gang members already have extensive police records before they join. The police submission to the ministerial inquiry into violence gives powerful evidence of the disastrous background factors in the lives of these multiple offenders, whose records often begin in their early teens, probably after some years of living outside parental control and supervision. Since no one cared, they may have grown up beyond moral and social constraint, and feel they owe nothing to a society that gave them nothing. The gang may be their first positive humanising social experience. We need to remember that gangs are not violent most of the time, and that the violence arises for structural reasons and in critical incidents.

The media tend to concentrate on the violent activities of some gangs or gang members as though membership is the cause of offending (108). Many of these individuals would have pursued these kinds of activities whether or not they were members of gangs. All multiple rape is not committed by gangs. It occurred throughout history long before modern gangs emerged. It is a sad fact of bad male behaviour in groups. But there is no doubt that the members of one particular gang have been associated with homicide and severe brutalities in the past and also with stand-over tactics to intimidate witnesses. Many gang houses maintain an arsenal of weapons of various kinds, chiefly in order to defend themselves against other gangs. The endeavours of the Labour Department through the contract work scheme and the employment of streetworkers specifically to deal with group employment has gone a long way to converting some of the gangs into skilled business operators. In some of these programmes examination has revealed evidence of featherbedding, contract inflation, the making use of every possible loophole and the taking advantage of poor supervision, but nothing specifically criminal has been revealed and that is not the general situation.

Gangs are frequently led by individuals with plenty of intelligence but little formal education, who have a sharp-edged underdog's view of society and are perfectly capable of finding dodgy ways of taking advantage of whatever the system allows. Techniques of intimidating government grant officers are not novel. Tom Wolfe vividly described similar methods for obtaining funds from grant officers under Lyndon Johnson's 'great society' programme. American society learnt years ago that gangs develop respect for a street-worker who is similar enough to themselves to be able to work with them, to call their bluff and to direct them away from socially disruptive and ultimately self-destructive activity (256).

Currently we have only the rudiments of such a service, no effective training technique for group and community workers, and therefore no way of offering alternatives to the effective recruitment practices which gangs operate both inside and outside the prison system. There is no doubt that gangs use the prison system to put their own recruitment officers inside and to offer a more effective bridge than the probation service for released prisoners. Your gang is more than your family; it will find you a lawyer if you are in trouble, give you money if you need it, provide for your entertainment, accommodation, even work should you want it. The surprising thing is that membership is only a few thousands. It is equally surprising that we have not learnt from the very techniques that gangs employ, how better to provide for those who are attracted to them.

For example, in some areas gangs have asked Maori communities for permission to build gang premises on papakainga (tribal land). In the cases of which we are aware, the kaumatua have not considered the marae to be the best place for gang living. There are thousands of hectares of tough country where the challenge of living communally and recreating the myth of a tribal past might be made to work and some have tried. But gangs are a product of urban life-style, the wage economy and the dole or other loose money in the system for those who would take advantage of it. Living rough in rural settings needs quite a different set of survival skills. If rural alternative life-styles are an answer someone will have to show how new skills will be learned and how people will be motivated to acquire them.

In any discussion of violence we must consider the world-wide phenomena of racial hatred and violence in holy or nationalistic crusades, rioting, terrorism, and political violence.

Prior to the 1981 Springbok tour, New Zealanders liked to think they had a riot-free history. But riot conditions were approached many times during the 1951 waterfront strike, and there were actual riots in Waihi in 1912 over industrial relations, in 1931 by the unemployed in Auckland, and in 1943 between US and New Zealand servicemen in the so-called battle of Manners Street. However, it was the Springbok tour that finally demonstrated that riotous violence is just an issue away from ordinary daily life.

Once the colonial wars destroyed Maori resistance in the 1870s, civil disobedience was rare. The extent and violence of the 1981 Springbok tour demonstrations are, therefore, very instructive. How was it that so many ordinary, peaceable citizens from all walks of life donned their own makeshift protective gear, linked arms, and advanced against trained squads of anti-riot police in such an unprecedented manner? Naturally, the media blamed the organisers and overseas influences, and the organisers, accepting that blame as tribute, blamed the police for the violence and the politicians for allowing the situation to arise in the first place.

Near riotous behaviour occurred on many occasions at this time, but there were incidents where the police lost their cool and such occasions became an opportunity for violent freeloaders to declare the kind of moral holiday which characterises a riot. The significant thing about the Springbok tour confrontations was that the protest was not organised by rabid lovers of violence, but by your friendly neighbourhood parish priests, the Boy Scout leader, the dean of the faculty, the secretary of the Christian Fellowship – indeed, by the very people who are the best organisers in society and do it all the time. It was the police, not the protestors, who looked to overseas models to find appropriate tactics and riot control gear.

There were several long-term consequences to the tour and its protests and confrontations. The police lost for ever their friendly neighbourhood 'bobby on the beat' image. In this generation they will never get it back. A new set of visual images of the police with armoured plastic defensive face-masks and headgear, long heavy woollen military-style protective coats, riot shields, and long batons is now part of many people's memory and perception of the police 'in action'. These images were a rude awakening; they connected what was going on here with images of Nazi shock troops, of race riots in Britain, the religious war in Northern Ireland, and political oppression in many parts of the world.

Perhaps we thought we lost an innocence we never really had, but what we gained was a new cynicism, a new dark dimension to our image of the police force. The riot gear became standard and ready for deployment, and community factions who favour repressive use of force were encouraged in their clamour. There is now a new image of the police in crowd control and for many it is a symbol of fear not of trust.

These factions, who speak of Empire, Freedom, Individual Rights, and Communist Subversion, who say they are pro-family, as if everybody else were not, are not as numerous as their media profile would imply. Their operations have been studied by Paul Spoonley, who points out that a small group of individuals keep inventing new organisations of which they are usually the only members (230). For some reason, much of this activity appears to be centred in Christchurch, although small fringe groups exist in the Wairarapa, Hawke's Bay, Wanganui, Northland, and other scattered locations.

Such groups have not reached the overt extremes of violence that we associate with the United States. As far as we know, they do not have arsenals stacked away, nor run guerrilla training courses. Their danger and their contribution to the politics of violence here is that they frighten the public, and encourage politicians to deal with violence in traditional ways which are known to be inadequate. The modern criminological consensus is that more police, longer sentences, and more punitive practices simply do not reduce violent offending and are, therefore, a waste of public money. They perpetuate the culture of violence in the land by supporting the ideology of violence.

Quite a different kind of riot erupted during a rock concert in Queen Street, Auckland, in December, 1984. Here, police intervened to stop a young persons' concert in the early evening which had been sponsored by the Auckland City Council to mark the end of the school year. The holiday atmosphere turned sour when the police attempted to stop men standing on verandahs from urinating on those below. Beer cans and bottles were thrown, and a full-scale riot erupted, reminiscent of European football stadiums, or the streets of Belfast. For days, television replayed the fifteen or so seconds of the most violent activity, cementing into public consciousness those images of street warfare. As one young participant commented (on radio), 'It was choice, just like television.' Suddenly television became reality – or did reality become TV?

Nobody set this trap. No one is to blame. It was a cultural phenomenon designed by the elements of a New Zealand pattern of violence. It has not happened since, but we could write a formula for it to happen again. The elements are: release from the restrictions of authoritarian control (e.g., high school); high alcohol use; a euphoric crowd with a few males acting like alpha-prime apes; inject a knee-jerk response by the coercive agencies of control (police); block off alternate informational or control mechanisms (e.g., tell the band to stop playing); instruct people to do something that they do not want to do and have no intention of doing (go home), because that is not what they came to hear; add a festival.

Naturally there had to be a public inquiry which at least cleared some of the public's scapegoats. In his report on the riot, Peter Mahon QC emphasised the role of unrestricted alcohol consumption (the containers also became convenient missiles), the unsuitable venue, poor police information and communication, the frustration when the police stopped the band (DD Smash) from playing, and the crudity of riot-control measures as the police tried to clear the concert venue. He put aside wider consideration of what he termed 'sociological factors', namely the conditions young people were experiencing in 1984, outside the event (136).

The police were not blameless, but it was not gangs, unemployment or communist subversion that instigated that Queen Street riot. It was the bad behaviour of drunken larrikins that acted as a catalyst for violence by too many people crowded into an inappropriate setting for a Friday night on the town. Caught up in the excitement and the action, a great many young people were carried along and behaved in an uncharacteristic and unthinking manner, and then sat around stunned afterwards wondering what had happened. If we do not learn to understand our capacity for violence we will never understand why it overtakes seemingly non-violent people.

The pattern of anti-authority, anarchist, and pro-violence themes prominent in youth culture, and especially in the lyrics of some 'heavy metal' rock groups, are part of this scene. People delude themselves when they think that Auckland is rather like Los Angeles, but a few decades behind. Auckland is like Los Angeles yesterday, as close as the latest satellite transmission of the most recent themes or events in youth culture. That is what Marshall McLuhan meant by the 'global village', linked in instantaneous electronic awareness and influence (133).

Political terrorism can erupt anywhere. Through the publicity given to terrorist activities, what appears to be copy-cat terrorist violence has already occurred at least three times in New Zealand (albeit on a very small scale): the *Rainbow Warrior* affair in 1985; the parcel-bomb murder of a Dunedin solicitor in 1962; and the briefcase bomb killing of a Wellington Trades Council official in 1984. Although these were of the do-it-yourself kitchen-bomb variety, they should not be discounted. Most terrorists use similar techniques. We should be aware, and take careful note, of the nature of terrorist activities elsewhere. It has happened here.

A great deal has been written about the use of terrorism for political ends. Within Europe, the hard core who commit terrorist acts appears numerically tiny – probably not more than two hundred people. They not only form a network, but are also highly mobile so that their strike-and-escape tactics confuse local and national security jurisdictions. These people are well funded, not only by their own blackmail activities but also within the covert political underworld. There are two kinds of terrorist. The first is the hired gun whose political motivations coincide with someone else's desire to organise a kidnapping or an assassination. In the second category are the fanatics who have come to regard their life as expendable for 'the cause'. The latter are not always wild-eyed fanatics, but would include the Belfast street-kid who has never known anything but political violence and has seen death so many times that he or she expects little of life anyway.

In New Zealand, it is hard to separate the paranoia from the reality. IRA fund-raisers have visited this country, appealing to the New Zealand population of Irish descent to support them in 'the troubles'. A small pro-PLO and anti-Israel lobby exists in this country and, although they do not advocate violence, they are supporting those who do. Some gang members too have such loyalty to the gang that they might hold their own life cheap. But we know of no one who would be prepared to take or risk life in defence of the ideologies of any existing New Zealand political party! There *are* issues here which might inspire terrorist violence. The anti-abortion lobby has an extreme fringe which has used arson, intimidation, and other terrorist tactics. Supporters of the South African white government may constitute a danger. Environmental issues occasionally become heated. But it is around racial issues that the greatest danger lies.

Some ultra-right extremists believe that Maori people are being subverted by overseas agencies, initially, it was claimed, in Cuba and more recently in Libya and the Middle East. We have talked with some Maori who have travelled to Cuba, Libya, and Nicaragua about what they learned there. They speak of the continuing effects of neo-colonial exploitation, about the difficulties of sustaining co-operative action amongst those liberated from, or currently subjected to, oppression. They learnt techniques of working with people to build communities rather than bombs to destroy them. They learnt how to use traditional culture to motivate people to embrace change. So far as we know, they did not learn where to buy rifles or other weapons of guerrilla warfare or how to booby-trap cars or construct parcel bombs. Such information is readily available to anyone who wants it, anyway.

The Third World and the Fourth World (that is, underdeveloped and oppressed minorities within developed countries) have no monopoly of political and terrorist violence. Indeed, terrorism is sustained by the arms industry, and the nuclear threat, as well as by commercial colonialism and monopoly. All these factors have influence here. We should not, therefore, except that New Zealand will, in the future, be free from the violence that occurs elsewhere in our world.

Every kind of violence that occurs elsewhere occurs here. We need to reduce the sources of violence in our own country, and protect ourselves as best we may from the external influences that might trigger violence here, but never lose sight of the violence that is within us all.

*Origins of New Zealand Violence*

# 6

# Socialisation and Social Control

The ultimate responsibility for violence in our society rests on each one of us. Violence is embedded in the culture patterns which we pass from generation to generation through socialisation, education, and participation.

One such pattern is the dangerous belief that violence is the result of irresistible impulse, which somehow places it outside individual responsibility and social control. Violence is not an impulse, but the channelling of 'state of arousal' energy towards a person or object. The doctrine of irresistible impulse is a dangerous but widely believed fiction which is often cited in justification. It even had a place in Napoleonic law where the defence of *crime passionnel* could be advanced in court, and is conceptually linked to notions of biological determination.

But it is opportunity, as well as urge, that sparks the violent attack. Opportunities for violence constantly surround us, as do media and other stimuli to violence. We must understand why we persist in offering patterns and models of violence which induce people to act violently.

On the one hand, we show considerable social disapproval, even horror, of violence in most of its forms. But on the other hand, we give children war toys, and encourage competitiveness and aggressive games which use the language of annihilation. As children grow up they see powerful individuals in the family and in society using or condoning violence, and less powerful individuals expressing personal power in a variety of ways. We all grow up, therefore, in a world of ambivalence.

There are several consequences of this confusion. Confronted by violence in others, we may be paralysed. Confronted with the temptation to be violent, we may feel justified by that past history of social approval. Given the chance, we may choose the violent alternative because that is the independent, autonomous and, therefore, individually powerful thing to do.

We are also induced into the ideology of instinct and irresistable impulse, which presents us with a peculiar dilemma. We may use it to justify our intimidation of others, but at the cost of having to permit to others the same licence against ourselves.

Confronted with double messages, human beings try to simplify. Thus, a person who has problems controlling anger may attempt to make anger a virtue, justify its use as a strategy, imply that it is temperament and leave others to make their accommodation. Gender polarity and stereotyping ascribe anger and violence to men but not to women. Such simplification provides neat dichotomies of victim and aggressor, dominant and dominated.

For twenty-five years, we have been researching patterns of child training in New Zealand families, both Maori and Pakeha, urban and rural (182, 184, 185, 186, 191, 192, 193, 194, 199, 200, 203). In our 1963 survey of child-rearing practices we included a number of questions on discipline and control (192). We were surprised by the major features which emerged from these data. New Zealand mothers relied on very few of the wide range of possible control techniques. Those they did use were, for the greater part, negative – scoldings, threats, reprimands, and punishment. Not only did they make infrequent use of positive or reward techniques but had very negative attitudes toward them, regarding them as bribes or evidence of 'spoiling', and, not infrequently, expecting that good behaviour should be its own reward. Finally, physical punishment was a moral obligation in, and criterion of, good parenting in the 1960s. The first principle of parenting was 'spare the rod and spoil the child', not 'suffer little children to come unto me'.

This is, of course, retrospective survey data in which respondents, notoriously, tend to present themselves in the best possible light. It may be that these levels of physical punishment were inflated by the naïve desire of our respondents to convince us that they took the burdens of parenthood seriously. They may not actually have punished as often as the survey claims but they certainly wanted us to think that they did.

Fifteen years later we repeated the survey (185). While many features of parent–child interaction and relationship appeared to have improved over this period of time, physical punishment persisted as the major pillar of parent control. Indeed, although the percentage of mothers who never used physical punishment increased from 1 to 10 per cent, 54 per cent of the mothers in the

1977 study used physical punishment at least weekly, compared to 35 per cent fifteen years before. Neither chance nor sampling differences can explain an increase of this magnitude. However, although mothers were now using physical punishment more frequently, they were less likely to regard it as effective. Only 14 per cent of the 1977 group found it unequivocally effective compared to 41 per cent of the earlier sample. Why then did they continue to do it if most thought it ineffective?

In 1963 only mothers were interviewed. Our 1977 study included fathers as well (185). Fathers appeared on the surface to use the same amount of physical punishment as mothers; however, because they spent less time with their children, their overall rate of physical punishment per contact hour must be greater. And almost twice as many fathers (one in four) as mothers thought physical punishment always worked, and another 50 per cent regarded it as quite effective most of the time. Fathers obviously felt more morally justified than mothers in using physical punishment, since 50 per cent of them considered they were doing the right thing compared to only 29 per cent of the women. Women were much more likely than the men to feel guilty and bothered by the use of physical punishment.

Mothers smacked their sons and daughters equally often, but fathers punished their sons more frequently than their daughters. When they punished their daughters, they were more likely to feel guilty about it. Fathers of sons were much more convinced that they were doing the right thing when they physically chastised them. Daughters responded with hurt feelings when hit by their fathers; sons responded with anger. The fathers reported fewer reservations about the effectiveness of physical punishment with their daughters; boys were punished more frequently and the punishment was considered less effective.

In 1987 we carried out a third study of child-rearing practices, in which the general patterns persisted. Fewer mothers in 1987 than in 1977 had never hit their child (2 per cent as compared with 10 per cent) and about half continued to hit their child at least once a week. More mothers now felt guilty about hitting, but they were also more likely to feel that physical punishment was effective. Fewer fathers, as well, had never hit their child (4 per cent in 1987 compared to 8 per cent in 1977). Fathers continued to find physical punishment effective in 1987, but more felt guilty about using it (191).

These data derive from interviews with parents of four-year-olds and reflect the foundation pattern, although many people think that as the child grows older, the need for physical punishment decreases. Even the mothers of the four-year-olds implied this, when they stated their belief that you cannot reason much with a preschool child. But we have data which shows that the pattern of control by physical force does persist into the teenage years; without it, many parents would see their authority in jeopardy.

In 1979 we devised a questionnaire that could be easily understood by twelve- and thirteen-year-olds and administered it to 110 Form II pupils in a Hamilton intermediate school (204). After a pilot survey, the questionnaire was produced in pencil and paper multi-choice form, thus reducing experimenter bias in interviewing techniques and in categorisation. The sample contained equal numbers (55 each) of males and females.

A wide range of questions concerning family authority and discipline was included. The first surprise was that there were differences in the replies of the boys and the girls concerning who exercised discipline within the family. For the boys there was no clear pattern – for a third it was mostly the mother, for another third the father, and for the rest it was both. But for the girls it was either the mother who exercised discipline, or both parents equally. However, from whatever direction the discipline came, the children were confronted with parental agreement about it. The parents backed each other up.

On the form of discipline used, there was little difference between the reports of the boys and the girls. The most frequent form of discipline was verbal (scoldings, growlings, and threats) with actual smacking and threats of deprivation of privileges coming high on the list.

How many of the twelve- and thirteen-year-olds were currently being smacked by either parent? For the girls, 40 per cent were still smacked by their mothers, and 36 per cent by their fathers. For the boys, 34 per cent were still smacked by their mothers and 51 per cent by their fathers. These seemed to us to be very high percentages. Many of the reasons which parents give for smacking very little children ('they don't understand', or 'teach them young') simply do not apply to children at these ages who presumably could now understand and who have certainly learned little from past treatment of this kind.

And how frequently did this happen? A third of the boys and a quarter of the girls were hit by one parent or both 'once a month' or 'more often'. These figures showed a considerable reduction from the percentage of four-year-olds (75 per cent) who were hit as frequently by their parents. However, these children were teenagers, well on the way to adulthood, and they were still being hit with considerable regularity in the pattern and in the places where they were hit as children – legs, bottoms, hands. We think that is degrading for all concerned.

The data suggested that since they were being hit for the most part with the parental hand, this was not premeditated punishment but simply 'lashing out'. However, fathers were more likely than mothers to use weapons such as straps and sticks. Some parents just picked up whatever was nearest and started hitting their child with it. The children mentioned such items as a hearth brush, shoes, slippers, belts, newspapers, wooden spoons, and garden hoses.

For what type of misbehaviour were the children punished in this way? For both sexes, general disobedience was the most frequent crime, but insolence came a close second, especially when girls were cheeky to their mothers. Aggression, bad language, carelessness, and staying out or being late were the other behaviour categories for which parents physically punished.

Notice that these misdemeanours all work one way – that is, there is no adult equivalent to a child's being cheeky or disobedient or using bad language. No one punishes parents for being cheeky or disobedient or for staying out late or not eating their vegetables. In some circumstances bad language may be legally proscribed but in many situations it is permitted; indeed in most ordinary daily settings it is not at all remarkable. It may be very unwise to be insolent to a police officer and possibly punishable if one deliberately disobeys instructions, but in adult relationships there is no criminal equivalent to being cheeky.

A quarter of the children in the sample were hit hard enough for it to hurt. They also wanted to hit back but dared not. Only a tiny percentage felt sorry for what they had done (7 per cent of the boys, 16 per cent of the girls). Maybe when they were little they could accept the pain and humiliation as matter of daily fact, but this is not the case at twelve or thirteen. Now resentment will simmer, grudges will be haboured, hate nursed.

Most of these children did not think smacking did any good. They knew they could expect it to occur for certain behaviour, but they continued to behave in those ways in spite of the likelihood of punishment.

Overall, our data showed that both the parents and the twelve- and thirteen-year-olds agreed that physical punishment was an ineffective method of changing behaviour. But parents continued to smack, and children continued to expect to be smacked. In fact, some children have told us that they would rather be smacked than be deprived of privileges or have something taken away from them. Both parents and children seemed to feel it 'clears the air' and reduces the tension that has built up between them. We think that this is one of the persistent myths about punishment, but also that it may be a prophecy that is self-fulfilling rather than empirical.

A study of eighty-eight third and fourth form girls and boys, ages thirteen and fourteen, conducted in 1980 by our students, revealed that one-third of these adolescent boys were still being hit by their mothers and 43 per cent by their fathers (196). Only 20 per cent of the girls were still being physically punished by either parent.

Interestingly, their parents were far less likely to report that they physically punished their teenage children. These data confirmed previous findings that boys were more likely to be physically punished than were girls, and more likely to be punished by their fathers than by their mothers. That young people of this age were still being physically punished for misdemeanours was yet another demonstration of the heavy reliance by New Zealand parents, particularly fathers, on violent methods of discipline and control (197).

We decided to follow this research with a survey of sixth form students, male and female, in Hamilton schools. Slightly more boys (some 24 per cent) than girls (21 per cent) reported that they had been subjected to physical punishment during their teenage years. The persistence of this pattern will come as a surprise to those who think that parents only hit little children. Some parents will hit anyone who opposes their authority. Violent men, especially, will be violent whenever their fragile controls are threatened (188).

In a sample of parents of children in one Hamilton primary school, 96 per cent of the fathers and 89 per cent of the mothers agreed with the statement 'that in certain circumstances it is all right for a parent to smack a child'. Hitting children is obviously considered to be a basic parental right and it is, therefore, not surprising that whenever we have publicly attacked section 59 of the Crimes Act (1962) which supports this right, the reaction has ranged from incredulity to vehement hostility. Even when parents have a genuine interest in other methods of control and might wish to reduce their dependence on physical punishment, they are reluctant to see any change in the law that would reduce this fundamental right. Many parents speak of physical punishment as the last resort and do not wish to be deprived of what they regard as the ultimate weapon.

As we reported in *Spare the Rod*, Sweden removed a similar right to hit children in 1966, and in 1979 went further and prohibited such punishment by parents (197). Some, no doubt, will continue to hit children, but the full moral weight of the legislatively endorsed Parenthood and Guardianship Code is against their doing so. There are no penalties (other than those for common assault), but there is a Children's Ombudsman and children can and do lay complaints.

From all the research data it is clear that New Zealand children grow up in a climate in which many of them are subjected to violence on a daily or weekly basis.

Our critics frequently ask us why we call smacking children a violent action. That question in itself is diagnostic of the sickness of our society. Violence is the use of force to get your own way, and that is essentially the way the Crimes Act (1962) defines an assault. The Act, however, provides in section 59 a let-out for parents and teachers. The revision of the Crimes Act, still under discussion at the time of writing, will remove the exemption for teachers but continue to protect parents. Notice, however, that the Crimes Act does *not* say that the act of striking a child is a different *kind* of act if performed by a parent. It simply says that this same act shall not, in those circumstances, be considered a crime. Again, this is a diagnostic indicator. The Crimes Act is saying, as our critics and indeed society itself are saying, that the same act is violent whenever it occurs, but that parents and teachers are allowed to be violent in this way. Why do they say this?

The answer goes right to the heart of our concepts of authority and control. In our culture, when we give someone authority over someone else, we have also, traditionally, given them the right to use force to exert that authority. 'What', most New Zealanders would say, 'is wrong with that?' We answer that it is unnecessary, harmful, and leads to individuals who have problems with authority.

Some parents believe that physical punishment within the authority of parenthood is justified by love; that it is justified because, without physical punishment, the child would never learn control. Therefore, they believe that what they are doing as parents ultimately benefits and protects the child. Such beliefs are incorrect. Self-control is not learnt by punishment. Instead, the victim learns either to emulate the punisher or to achieve his or her purposes by being meekly submissive, sneaky, and devious.

The other reason many New Zealand parents persist in this pattern is that they believe it is their duty to control children, and the more directly and obviously they do this, the better parents they are. They point to children who go 'off the rails' as an object lesson in what happens if parents do not teach their children self-control. We would agree, entirely. Children who grow up without an environment of love, attention, and concern are tragically deprived of all that they need to become fulfilled and functioning members of society. This is neglect, and neglect is a form of abuse. Children are entitled to learn all that they are capable of learning in an environment of care and understanding. Such an environment precludes the use of physical force or psychological means of coercion.

If we really seek to raise individuals who will exercise control over themselves, we must not subject them to arbitrary control which they have no rational way of understanding, because the motives are either hidden or confused with love. We believe that adequate reasons should always be given to a child of any age, as such reasoning will not only develop language competence, but also develop self-control by rationality. This begins by informing the child of the consequences of conduct before it occurs, or by explaining them after the event, and by rewarding any behaviour which conforms to socially valuable patterns.

With very young children, parents have to depend upon what

psychologists call contingency management, that is, managing the environment so that the child is less likely to engage in activities which the parents find undesirable or which may harm the child. Children do not need to learn right from wrong by performing wrong actions – that is absurd. When a child performs the right action, long before the behaviour is under verbal control, he or she can appreciate the parental approval, warmth, and satisfaction, and the smooth movement through chains of behaviour which are undisrupted by punishment or disapproval. What the wise parent is seeking is to strengthen the capacity of the child to make the 'right choices' and to begin to understand the concept of right choices. Behaviour that is developed in this way is disciplined but is under the control of the developing child.

Children who are physically punished come to have a negative view of themselves as well as of the punisher. In the jargon of corrective social work, they have a poor self-image. Their sense of self is not built upon a wide range of skills and strategies or general social competence; instead they are forced to adopt a reactive either aggressive or submissive manner to overcome these limitations. Frequently, they will know exactly how to provoke an authoritarian response, since to do so precipitates a confrontation in which, even if they lose, they may feel that they either did so with honour or, at the very least, made the other person lose face by forcing them into irrational action. The only corrective to negative self-image is to bring the individual slowly back onto a gradient of success and the development of competence.

Parents who are likely to know, to guess and to understand what lies behind the challenges that their children confront them with have some chance of dealing with negative components in the self image of young people. Teachers will have more difficulty because they are often ignorant of the background forces and histories and have to handle too much behaviour by too many people all at once. Nevertheless, teachers in training, and through in-service training, can role play such situations and prepare in other ways so that they are not thrown by the often skilful tactics of some children who will take every situation as a way of challenging authority if they can.

An abused child may grow into a violent person who may be the very last to admit to anything negative about himself or herself. Yet the truth of the matter is that the violent behaviour itself may arise from deep inner feelings of self-hate or poor self-esteem, projected out upon the society that, in the view of that person, did not offer him or her a chance.

# 7

# Institutional Violence

The organisation and structure of all our social institutions must be examined to detect ways in which they may sustain and perpetuate the patterns which lie behind violence. No institution can be exempted since all have to deal with the cultural patterns that determine violent expressions or events. Hospitals, schools, debating chambers, agencies of social justice or welfare, universities, sporting organisations, churches – all must be audited and monitored. When individuals act outside the institutional framework they may do so in ways that are broadly acceptable, in which case we regard them as creative people, or loners, and their actions may have the effect of bringing about change within the institutions themselves. They may set out to do this deliberately and become activists or campaigners. But there are others who, by acting outside the framework, come to be labelled criminal or delinquent.

Institutions claim to sustain basic values and their purposes are, therefore, moral almost by definition. But the institutions themselves have been shaped by layers of history and do not always do what their charters say they should. Like individuals, institutions have hidden agendas because neither their structures nor their statements of intent are entirely rational.

For example, there is considerable literature on how medical students go through a process of 'secondary socialisation' – that is, of learning how to act like doctors and thus fit into the role that history and society have fashioned for that profession (43, 57). The overt charter of this socialisation is the Hippocratic oath to protect and preserve life. But this process also creates less noble attitudes, such as those which made it possible for medical researchers to deny women appropriate treatment for incipient cancers and to behave autocratically towards other medical staff and patients alike (31, 32, 42). It is the structure of the institution of medicine which sustains these behaviours and provides the rewards and satisfactions that maintain them. Much as one might put one's effort into changing the behaviour of a particular doctor, the structure of the institution works against change.

In the matter of violence, there is no institution, not even the military, which condones the unrestricted use of force against the person of another. There are, however, circumstances, and we will examine them, in which particular institutions condone the use of force to achieve ends which are considered socially desirable. In this chapter we will show how violence has become built into the structure of the institutions of social control in ways which positively sanction actions inconsistent with the generally accepted moral principle of peaceable intent and action.

The conflict between overt rejection and covert acceptance of force and violence in controlling behaviour places enormous strains upon those least able to resolve the dilemma. There are whole categories of individuals – for example, those who are economically, educationally or intellectually disadvantaged – who may respond to frustration and strain by recourse to violent solutions. Similarly, there are individuals whose personal history and experience of violence have made them likely to deal with conflict by forceful means.

We have already discussed the social foundations of violence in general family patterns. These become the more potent and entrenched when the individual is growing up in a social context where violent actions are condoned by institutions, for example, in the more overtly violent gangs or socially oppressed subgroups.

At a time when the nature of schools and schooling is changing, it is appropriate to ask what the roles of educational institutions have been in sustaining violence. Historically, the concern for excellence has led to a concentration on competitiveness, fear of failure, punishment for failure, and a pedagogy that empowered teachers and disempowered everyone else. Thus many parents felt alienated, and so too did those children who failed to comply with the standards of the school or its system of sanctions. Schools were not experienced as punitive institutions by those children who accepted the authority of the teacher, aspired to the school's social and intellectual goals, acted with emotional control, had verbal fluency (in English), and assisted the teacher in maintaining the culture of the classroom. But children who did not fit this mould were punished, either physically, or indirectly by withdrawal of privilege, praise, emotional warmth, or the other rewards that sustain the system. A 'successful' teacher might, in fact, be using these indirect punitive controls in ways that have devastating effects upon some children, whose understandable reaction is to hate both the context and the persons who so alienate them. We do not know of any research which has counted the number of children who have become alienated in this way by the schooling system. But we know that there are many who leave as soon as they lawfully can.

As parents and administrators set out to restructure the education system they will have had to confront many questions, but we doubt that there will be many who have asked themselves, 'How can we make the environment of this school so *enjoyable* that children would wish to stay here for as long as they possibly can on any day, in any term, and over the years?'

Teaching is a nurturing process. It is the management of the resources of learning, and the rewards for having learned, in ways that are precisely tuned to the developmental needs and readiness of individual children. There is, therefore, no real distinction between learning and growth. However, none would sensibly imagine that growth can be promoted by competition, ridicule, shaming or punishment of any kind.

The experience of children in preschool and primary schools is generally more positive than in secondary schools; the learning styles are more relaxed and physical punishment is much less likely. Preschools, with the exception of kohanga reo, outlawed physical punishment from their earliest days and all have relied upon a nurturant style of teaching which our society traditionally associates with women. Indeed these centres, and also many primary schools, are predominantly run and staffed by women.

It is after primary school that a reduction in the nurturant atmosphere occurs. This is correlated with an increase in the proportion of male teachers who, according to gender stereotype, are less likely to value close personal attention to and emotional involvement with the learner. This is coupled with an increase in the number of teachers experienced by each child, which reduces opportunities for empathy and mentoring.

Male teachers have always been the chief barrier to the elimination of physical punishment, either because they believe in its effectiveness or because they are afraid to have what they believe to be a powerful tool taken from them (40). It is not, in fact, a tool of learning, but a tool of control by coercion. If you believe in physical punishment you believe, by definition, in the right of one individual to coerce another.

In 1984 the Labour Party manifesto promised the unqualified abolition of physical punishment in all schools. After six years this had still not been achieved. Why did this not happen forthwith? Responsibility must lie with the caucus and cabinet who failed to support the then minister of education, Russell Marshall when he attempted to implement a party policy decision. The implementation would have cost nothing, in financial terms. The party, however, considered such enactment would be too far ahead of public opinion and the caucus responded to the public, rather than to the party. This delay reveals the strength of the institutional framework with which we are dealing; physical punishment is firmly entrenched within the New Zealand psyche (197). But by merely banning the strap or stick you do not thereby abolish the basis of such punitive practices in school culture.

The culture of the school is not carried by teachers alone nor fashioned only by formal charters. When we surveyed sixth form students in Hamilton high schools, we found that the boys, who were more likely than the girls to be the recipients of corporal punishment, were also more likely to endorse its use. Two options for gender equality were offered in the survey form: abandoning physical punishment altogether, or hitting girls as well as boys. Girls opted for the former, while boys were more likely to choose the latter, showing the extent of male socialisation into acceptance of physical punishment by the sixth form.

One positive finding, however, emerged from the survey: the boys from a coeducational high school that had long ago abandoned corporal punishment were much less likely to endorse the practice than the boys from the schools where it still continued.

No one knows the extent of classroom bullying or playground violence, although teachers, particularly male teachers opposed to the abolition of physical punishment, frequently argue that this is one behaviour that will only respond to corporal punishment. The moral precept here seems to be that one must meet violence with violence, aggression with oppression, and that the Old Testament dictum of an eye for an eye has proven its efficacy and moral primacy over any other method dealing with aggression. If, in three thousand years of the Judeo-Christian tradition, this practice has not worked, surely it is time to find out why our society is so reluctant to abandon it.

It is more than a little ironic that the most passionate defenders of physical punishment from a religious quarter are Christian fundamentalist groups. Christ himself engaged in only one violent activity that we know of, namely driving the money-lenders from the temple, and specifically called upon the Jews of his day to reject the notion of a punitive God and embrace a doctrine of peace, love and good will.

It is from those who followed this doctrine that social reforms to achieve a less violent society have largely stemmed: the Quakers and the anti-slavery movement, the Shaftesbury era of social reform in Britain, Jane Addams in Chicago, and the other pioneer women who began the profession of social work. Early feminists found it necessary to reassess their position as Christians and to remind people that Christ was kind to prostitutes and surrounded himself with sympathetic women.

In New Zealand, the Christian force behind Project Waitangi, the anti-apartheid movement, Amnesty International, and the Christian Coalition for Peace, Freedom and Justice has been substantial and politically effective. Without it, the nuclear-free policy and the redirection of foreign policy and aid to recognise and emphasise the work of voluntary and volunteer agencies in recent times would not have occurred. But Christians themselves are constantly in danger of being hijacked by the fundamentalists – the 'terrorists' of the Judeo-Christian tradition – who cling to the notion of a vengeful God standing ready to strike terror into the hearts and minds of transgressors.

The power of the fundamentalist lobby to capture the political centre was clearly demonstrated in the debate on the Homosexual Law Reform Bill which became law in 1986. Though the Bill was eventually passed, the legislative process was prolonged over months of debate. MPs were subjected to a write-in campaign. The Select Committee process was flooded with objections and considerable publicity given to a questionable petition. All of this was defended as democracy in action yet the opinion polls showed an over-all majority of the public favoured reform. In the end the clauses protecting homosexuals from discrimination were dropped. Homosexual relationships challenge the traditional nuclear family which is the structural model for many institutional relationships in our society. Such public controversy reflects all the schisms, structural weaknesses and fractures, vested and self-interests, and implicit and covert values of a society. This one centred around gender, sexuality, and power – which also triangulate the nature of violence.

Lest we appear to be harsh on fundamentalist Christians we should add that all forms of religious fundamentalism raise exactly these issues. Commentators such as Robin Morgan argue that it is no accident that the present resurgence of fundamentalism in its many forms follows a period of unprecedented advancement for women (157). While we may be aware of the effects of Zionist fundamentalism in Israel, of Islam in Iran and Malaysia, of Christian fundamentalism in Fiji, of reactionary Protestantism in South Africa or Northern Ireland, the same processes are occurring here at home. Such movements seek to establish an unquestioning and unnatural trust in an authority which is male in style and character. Nationalism and patriotism are also essential ingredients in such movements.

Religious fundamentalism is only one part of the so-called 'new right', which encompasses many groups within our society who call for a return to fundamental principles. Spoonley has identified the political right and assessed its present strength (230). Whereas it was once thought that the political right was numerically tiny in relationship to the stridency of its message, that view obscures the degree to which substantial numbers of New Zealanders will leap upon any bandwaggon that offers simplistic slogans. For the new political right the slogans are individualism, freedom of choice, freedom from state interference, a laissez-faire stance on economic affairs, and a naive faith that enlightened self-interest will bring about every kind of social advancement that might be regarded as necessary and desirable. The new right reifies enlightened self-interest into a natural law which it calls 'market forces' and to which its adherents attribute ultimate authority. 'Market forces' translates as 'economic self interest' (without any preceding qualification that it might be 'enlightened'). Social interest is fudged over by appeals that the people (politicians, economists, financiers, industrialists) involved are not monsters and by some kind of inherent motivation 'naturally' will attend to the public interest once they have money enough to do so. In the interim, what is supposed to happen to the general fabric of social welfare is not altogether clear but targeting and means testing and benefit reduction are all involved.

It may not be the fault of the economic right that our society in recent years has seen unleashed upon it a band of unscrupulous speculators, financial manipulators and a generation who operate at the outer limits of what is financially legal (and beyond it safely undetected). But whatever produces the correlation, when there is a rise in the power of the economic right, watch also for an increase in corruption, poverty, the concentration of wealth in fewer hands, and a dismissive attitude towards social violence. When the poor see themselves shut out from wealth and opportunity, increasing numbers will seek to take what they need – isn't that what free enterprise is all about? Crime must be seen within the context of the prevailing ideology; it is not alien to it but committed by those alienated from it.

The adversarial style of parliament may have been modified by select committee procedures which were supposed to provide calmer and more rational discussion and more public participation. Perhaps they have succeeded to some degree, but the select committees themselves are still subject to belligerent attacks upon witnesses, adversarial debates between politicians, and manipulative brokering of information – they are not even obliged to share the information they have with those appearing before them. The power remains with cabinet, not with the select committee.

If people are not empowered to participate meaningfully in the political process, their rights may be violated and their sense of oppression will increase. However, because parliament is under the constant scrutiny of the media, and therefore very public, violations of personal or group rights are not easy to conceal. The more decentralised the exercise of power, the more tempting it may be to avoid responsibility for those rights. Current government attempts to make administration more regional may achieve the opposite of what was intended, because local government politics are conducted by executive employees and council committees rather than in public arenas, and civic institutions are subject to convert agendas. They do not need to exercise the kind of force that is exercised by the police as an arm of central government, but they are agencies of control nevertheless. Planning departments, health inspectors, traffic officers, officers in charges of dog control, noise control, pollution control, and swimming pool fencing controls – all exercise control in the interests of the community. For the most part, that control is rational, efficient, necessary, and benevolent, and there are safeguards protecting civil and human rights. *Most* people experience *most* civic authority as non-authoritarian. But this does not mean that it always is.

The same ambivalent conclusion might be reached concerning police functions in New Zealand. New Zealanders, quite reasonably, want to live in a society where law and order prevail. But they believe that the way to achieve this is through increasing the coercive arm of the police and the capacity of society to punish offenders – a belief which reinforces authoritarian rather than responsible control.

In a series of National Research Bureau (NRB) polls in 1987, law and order outranked in importance all other issues except unemployment and the general state of the economy (*New Zealand, Herald*, 18 December 1987). In that year, the proportion of those surveyed who expressed anxiety about crime and public safety rose from 5 to 13 per cent. This was the year of the Ministerial Committee of Inquiry into Violence (the Roper Report). But by March 1990, concern about law and order was a top priority for only 3 per cent of those polled, outranked by concern about unemployment (49 per cent), the economy (14 per cent), government (9 per cent), racial problems (9 per cent), and moral climate and public morality (4 per cent) (*New Zealand Herald*, 3 March

1990). But even if crime figures were to take a downturn, the Commissioner of Police warns us, such a trend 'must not be seen as any justification for relaxing police or community activities in crime prevention' (*New Zealand Herald*, 18 December 1987).

The police in New Zealand are forced to carry an inordinate burden in both law enforcement and crime prevention, being the institution most conspicuously involved. The police are not just the front line, but frequently the only line of defence, because of failure to inhibit the aggressive and violent behaviour of young men, to deal more rationally with alcohol abuse, to deal with domestic violence on a community basis, to cut back the public display of violent and criminal activity as entertainment on television, videos, and movies, to confront the violent potential in what we call healthy sporting activity, and to control firearms.

We do not think that the New Zealand police force is in its recruitment, training, or methods, any more violent than any other police force elsewhere. It may, indeed, be better than many or even most. But the real issue is that the institutional framework of policing is not historically designed for prevention. The police in fact are not psychologists or sociologists or social planners, but are part of a mechanism of social control in a society which is more concerned with punishing the offender than with seeking to eliminate the causes of offending.

New policies emphasise community policing and sentencing, increased youth aid, neighbourhood watch, consultation with marae and iwi agencies, other consultation, negotiation and many welcome reforms. Both legislatively and internally, change is underway. Claims of institutional violence by the police force are hard to document and hard to sustain, especially when such reforms are advanced as counter-evidence. But a 'force' it is.

This brings us to the creaking apparatus of the justice system and, all too frequently, to the prison system. Compared with similar Western countries, New Zealand has a very high rate of imprisonment. Britain has the highest rate in Western Europe. New Zealand's is higher than that. Within our own society, there are those, including the Prime Minister, who have come to the conclusion that prisons do not correct or change behaviour for the better. Furthermore, taking the criminal out of the community allows the community to forget that he (or very occasionally she) exists and to continue to ignore the ways in which social processes contribute to criminal offending. But surely the community can do more than barricade its doors and windows? The origins of criminal offending are well known and have been frequently documented. We *do* know what society must do in order to reduce violent offending.

Most New Zealanders care very little about what kind of prisons we have so long as they are suitably punitive and not too comfortable and are located well away from their backyard. Successive commissions of inquiry, reports on the prison system, and secretaries and ministers of justice have recognised the futility of long sentences, which institutionalise the prisoner and are breeding grounds for criminal association, instruction and organisaton. Prisons are not deterrents, either, for those who live 'outside' in conditions of such social deprivation, personal violence, and misery that a return to prison may not be unwelcome. But the law-and-order lobby so intimidates the politicians that prison numbers increase, sentences lengthen, and reform becomes a tinkering at the periphery of the system.

Another reason is that there is a huge financial investment in the existing facilities, to say nothing of personal careers in the law and its enforcement.

The Ministerial Committee of Inquiry into the Prison System made some radical suggestions for reform (151). It suggested a series of regional, medium-security prisons to replace the current minimum and maximum security prisons, supplemented by a network of 'habilitation centres', so that the punitive and habilitative functions of a prison sentence could be clearly separated. Those who opted for habilitation would receive counselling and training at such centres.

Nevertheless the bars remain. They are not just on the windows of the prisons. They are around the minds of those who continue to believe that prisons should do what they clearly cannot.

To abandon or even reduce the prison alternative will involve a radical reallocation of public resources (both money, and personnel) away from current prison institutions to other social objectives. When the Roper Report on Violence (150) recommended more money for early childhood education, it acknowledged that people who are brutal become so in conditions where they were themselves brutalised. Yet to suggest the redirection of prison funding to, say, the prevention of child abuse is to risk ridicule. Later (Chapter XV), we will examine in detail possible social policies and programmes for crime reduction. In essence, all such programmes must act to break the cycle, either within a generation or between generations, that perpetuates the culture of offending.

# 8

# Violence in a Multi-cultural Society

Up until now we have been talking about New Zealand as though it contains only a single or dominant culture. This dominant culture carries an ideology of violence clearly demonstrated by its history, particularly in relation to cultural minorities. But there are many cultures living here beside the dominant one, and they have different ideologies relating to aggression and violence and different histories of cultural determination.

For example, Asian populations have always kept a low profile in this country, but their traditional diligence and hard work is demonstrated by success in education, business, and industry. They have a low frequency of criminal offending and, so far as we know, simply do not participate in the New Zealand culture of violence. While there are Asian forms of martial art, in the Western sense they do not box. Neither do they do play rugby; they do not join the armed forces. We have no statistical information on levels of domestic violence, but their traditional respect for elders and the roles ascribed to women sustain very stable family patterns.

For all their similarities of history and culture, Polynesian groups differ from one another in many respects, including the way in which aggression is expressed. There is a wide body of anthropological research information on this (194, 200, 203). Some researchers emphasise the difference between Eastern and Western Polynesia (217, 246). The Eastern cultures (Tahiti, the Marquesas, and the Cook Islands) are said to demonstrate patterns that inhibit the expression of aggression and require suppression of anger, whereas in Western Polynesia (Samoa, Tonga, Fiji, New Zealand) that is not so.

There are problems with this formulation. Both Hawaiian and New Zealand Maori cultures derive from Eastern Polynesia yet both have aggressive and warlike traditions. From his analysis of how emotions were handled in Tahiti, Levy showed that a pattern of suppression was also accompanied by violent outbreaks from time to time. Tahiti, indeed, seems to sustain both violent and non-violent patterns causing considerable interpersonal conflict (125). Oliver reports practices of infanticide and human sacrifice in traditional Tahiti which can scarcely be regarded as gentle (167).

A more meaningful distinction may be made between the high islands and the atolls. Atolls generally have tiny populations and, since there is nowhere else to go, the people are forced to maintain good relationships with one another. Atoll dwellers generally have to work harder and longer for their sustenance, and have never developed the cult of warfare with its tales of heroism and the aggrandizement of aggression (217). Borofsky gives an excellent example of the delicate internal diplomacy of disagreement in an atoll culture when he describes the negotiations involved in significant social change in Pukapuka (28). Blood sacrifice, human sacrifice and cannibalism are not found anywhere in the atolls of the Pacific, whereas the high islands almost all had such traditions prior to the arrival of Christianity.

The psychological dynamics of sacrifice and cannibalism are very similar in Polynesia, even though in the Pacific they never coexist in a culture. Traditional Maori society did not pursue elaborate ceremonial rituals of human sacrifice to the gods. Warfare was the central dynamic, not temple practice. But when the war was over, the consumption of human flesh was a highly significant ritual, close in character to the Hawaiian practice of offering flesh to the gods. The Hawaiians had elaborate temple ceremonies and priestly rituals in which animal and human sacrifice played important roles, but they did not eat their victims whose flesh was sacred to the gods alone. Hawaiian warfare was relatively local and unimportant until the rise of the Kamehameha dynasty and the domination of the islands by one ali'i family. Thus, the artefacts of Hawaiian history are ceremonial objects of sacrifice, whereas those of Maori history are more often the beautiful but deadly tools of battle (183).

All that is in the past. How does it relate to New Zealand now? From this background one would expect to find low rates of violence in recent immigrant groups from atoll cultures, such as the northern Cooks, the Tokelaus, and Niue. And this is the case. The Tongan, Samoan, and Maori traditions are more heroic, or more bloody, depending on your point of view. Tongans, Fijians, and Samoans, throughout their history, have fought with each other, and in modern times have maintained a strong identification with military and police institutions. These are cultures in which peaceableness was never particularly valued, and in which rivalry and contests over status were very important. There were quite elaborate institutional and ceremonial frameworks within which this rivalry could be expressed; for example, Kava ceremonies, status marriages, Maori oratory, Samoan gift-giving. There was also the lineal authority structure which was supposed to dampen down and resolve excessive rivalry. The modern adaption of these cultures has found new ways of expressing status rivalry which do not depend on warrior traditions no longer available or appropriate.

We have shown elsewhere how these Polynesian patterns of rivalry are established through the socialisation mechanisms of peer interaction and peer management of the learning process (194, 200, 203). Both the learning of an appropriate interpersonal style, as well as important dynamics such as group loyalty, and participation in consensus decision-making persist into the present and the New Zealand setting.

For all the disruption that has occurred in basic socialisation patterns, the strongest elements persist (200). Multiple parenting remains an important principle in Polynesian families. Respect patterns persist towards the old, religious pastors and consensus leadership. Intense in-group loyalties of the kind that peer groups foster can be seen in dozens of different kinds of Polynesian organisation, in Church groups and clubs, women's groups, language preschools, youth or gang structures, entertainment groups and especially in and around high schools where such groupings are encouraged and supported.

Throughout all Polynesian societies, high and low, old and new, status rivalry leads to respect behaviour (79, 225). The great justification given by Polynesian parents for the use of physical punishment in child rearing is the need to inculcate respect from the earliest age. And children who are hit hard at home find solace elsewhere, with other relatives or amongst their peers. The frequency of physical punishment in Polynesian families may seem surprising in cultures where small babies and toddlers are so valued and indulged and where great emphasis is placed on *aroha* and *aloha*, the ethic of love.

The Western Samoan consul, Mr Afamasaga Toleafoa, commenting on this matter, said:

> *Samoans certainly believe in some strict form of discipline which does include corporal punishment – I wouldn't call it violence. Parents do chastise their children if need be and they will administer the rod. But ninety per cent of the time it is done properly and with love* (New Zealand Herald, 5 November 1988).

These remarks were made in response to Felix Donnelly's claim that some Pacific Island cultures condone violence towards young people (53). The consul also asserted that verbal sanctions are more powerful than physical punishment in Samoan society. This may very well be true where the authority of the *matai* is secure and the social power he represents remains intact and effective. But Samoans are no more exempt than anyone else from the general consequences when the use of physical punishment is a substantial, if not the primary, method of control. The consul's admission, that in ten per cent of cases it is not done properly, is a clear indication that something should be done to change the situation. Just what, is of course a matter for Samoans to decide. But the need for changes to be made is clear.

A parallel case arises in respect of the use of corporal punishment in kohanga reo. New Zealand preschools have never used physical punishment, but the Maori language preschools, kohanga reo, have never adopted such a policy. We would like to know how many Maori people believe it is culturally acceptable. If the movement were to ban the practice each kohanga reo could then work to find alternative forms of control using appropriate cultural concepts and means. We have been told, by kohanga reo kuia, that the issuing of national edicts is not the Maori way, and of that we are well aware. But we think that Maori people should be made as aware as any others of the consequence of authoritarian use of coercive force (197).

Statements have been made to us by Polynesians of standing that physical punishment of children was not as common in pre-Christian days as it is now. When the authority of the church challenged the authority of the chiefs, a dangerous conjunction occurred. The mission influences which came to the South Pacific were mainly low-church Protestant and evangelical Catholic, rather than the more liberal and reforming religious forces at work in some places in Europe at the time. Two distinct authoritarian institutions thus reinforced each other. There were, of course, confrontations and contests for power and there were areas, such as the Waikato or Taranaki, where Christianity lost out altogether. In these two places a pervading ethos of peace was espoused after invasion and heavy warfare had destroyed the tribal systems. The prophets Te Whiti and Tohu preached doctrines of peace at Parihaka in Taranaki (181). In the Waikato, the prophet-king Tawhiao proscribed the use of arms after the land wars and made peaceableness a major prescription in Tariao, his syncretist religion of pai marire – 'the gentle way' (56).

From the outset, Maori culture was subjected to waves of violation by representatives of different European institutions, each of which had its own patterns of coercion. The early traders exploited and depleted resources and were frequently lawless, indulging in rape, pillage, and random slaughter. The advent of mercantile commerce required further resource capture, including that of labour and of land. Settler militias added to the destruction. Waves of epidemic swept through the indigenous population, who were denied access to medical services (111). The missionaries collaborated with and condoned many of these oppressive acts. They seized land themselves. They armed the natives. The Church blessed guns and armies. It was an arm of the state, just as the military was.

As we look at New Zealand history we see that many of those who oppressed Maori people were, indeed, individuals with violent traits. Some, like von Tempsky (171), were irrational and erratic. Some alternated between savagery and compassion, Grey for example (213), or were simply mercenaries.

This history of violent relationships between the Pakeha, the Maori and other Pacific Island peoples continues. We are calling upon all New Zealand cultures to conduct their own examinations and formulate their own agendas for change.

There have been a number of reports by the Policy Research Division of the Department of Justice in which Maori offending and the effects of the criminal justice system are considered (9, 46). The most recent, 'The Maori and the Criminal Justice System: He Whaipaanga Hou – A New Perspective', by Moana Jackson, declares violent offending to be a dehumanised and callous disregard for the inherent tapu of other people and a selfish, frequently destructive disregard for their property rights (103). The report links the violence of young Maori men to the violence done to their culture through colonialism. Since their traditional basis of control has been stripped away, these young men are plunged into the confusions of disturbed behaviour, mental illness, or violent crime.

The legal and social constraints of traditional Maori society were very strong, and remain so in those parts of the country where marae and tribal structures still operate. But these structures can no longer deal with those whose respect for them is limited or who reject them entirely. 'The Maori and the Criminal Justice System' outlines the basis upon which Maori law operated and calls for the reconstruction of such controls. What are they?

Basically, an individual in the Polynesian world is a member of a collectivity: a family, a whanau, a hapu, or a variety of optional groupings which, though they may no longer be based on kinship alone, function in a similar way (203). Many work trusts, urban group houses, and some gangs operate on these principles, and may reconstruct traditional social controls. The group might make recompense by gifts or payment to a person who is harmed, or to the family of the person assaulted or raped. The person who

commits the offence may be required to 'whakaiti' (humble) himself
or herself by some personal act of abasement, which might involve
performing services for a period of time for the victim and for the
group to which the victim belonged. The crime would be spoken
about in language more direct and plain than the ritualised phrases
of Pakeha justice; the retribution would be more immediate, direct,
and personal. The process of acknowledging the wrong, of
recompense for it, and of rehabilitation until forgiveness has been
earned is long and personally intense. The offender is be supported
as he or she proceeds through a culturally defined relearning
experience. Reconstruction of such a process would have to rest on
a kaupapa, or basis of Maori values. Let us consider the nature of
these.

**Figure 1**

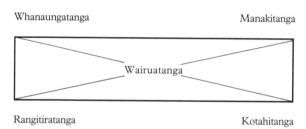

Whanaungatanga is the value placed upon family processes which
are based on kinship obligations. In principle, the collective has
primacy over the individual. In modern conditions, an individual
may have long lost contact with and knowledge of the whanau, or
family, structures to which he or she belongs. Jackson's point is that
although we assume that such alienation is permanent, inevitable,
and irreversible, this is not the case. Serious attempts to restore
whanau control over disruptive or lawless behaviour can and should
be made.

The whanau concerned may be less than pleasantly surprised to
learn that one of its members is a notorious bank robber and is now
to be returned to their care and control. The individual may have
little feeling of affection or obligation towards the family, or indeed
may have run to escape the claustrophobic social conditions that
some people experience in a closeknit Maori community. Jackson is
not proposing an easy alternative, yet it is one some Maori may
want to attempt.

Pakeha who think of this as a soft option fail to realise the long-
term severity of being sentenced to the continuing judgements of
your relatives. By comparison, prison may be the soft option. In

some ways prison is harsher on the families than on the offender
(46).

The second principle, which flows from the first, is one of
reciprocal care or manakitanga. Maori must feed and give emotional
and all other kinds of support to their kinsfolk, and no one counts
the quantities or costs. The word reciprocity is inadequate to
describe this value for it implies more than gift for gift. Manaki
means that the door is always open and the well of goodwill will
never run dry, no matter how harsh the judgement may be or the
suffering which one must go through.

These two principles bind together with a third which is the core
of both individual identity and group cohesiveness – the value
placed upon kotahitanga or feeling of unity, of being at peace and at
one together. Some see this as the highest value of all since it is so
difficult to achieve. Maori political process strives for consensus
through the recognition of the viewpoint of each individual; the
group would rather talk and wait interminably than force some
compromise solution which would alienate one of its members. A
dissident or a returning offender may need to state their case over
and over again until everyone is prepared to make allowance for
what they say or what they have done. The rehabilitation process is
quite unlike the Pakeha concept that, once guilt has been
established, a punishment price can be set upon it and then
discharged. In the Maori world, all sorts of later events may reflect
back upon the collective understanding of how great the guilt was
and what the price must be. It is unfortunate that the Maori social
mechanisms for maintaining this process have been undermined by
the Pakeha system and fallen into disuse. It will not be easy to
reconstruct them, but it is an alternative worth pursuing.

Ultimately, all three of these values depend upon the structure of
authority within the Maori world, that is, upon rangatiratanga.
Maori society is not egalitarian in the Pakeha sense but is infinitely
status graded. Each person has a right only to a specific place and
must behave accordingly or lose it. The structure of authority
depends upon significant acts that establish ascendency of one
person over another, but status is not fixed. Position must be
maintained and can be advanced. A person displays status or mana
by supporting, not punishing, by affirming, not ordering, by
humility, not arrogance. Pakeha have great difficulty understanding
rangatiratanga because Western notions of authority endorse
individuality.

Finally, all these values lock together in wairuatanga. It has
become a common vulgarism to translate this value as spirituality,
but to do so muddles up all the Christian associations of the Pakeha
with the Maori process of validating actions according to their

consistency with traditional principles. Wairuatanga is the principle of cultural integration that hold all things together over time; it is as material as it is metaphysical; as contemporary as it is ancestral.

For any of these cultural values we should not look for direct translation or simple formula phrases, but seek to understand the interrelated meanings that these principles have in Maori society and culture.

It is certainly possible, and quite practical, to take this value base and look at it as a way of generating a programme for reducing or preventing crimes of violence, for intervening when violence occurs, and for rehabilitating the violent offender.

There are some offences so outrageous that Maori communities may prefer not to deal with them. In the past, sexual violators or murderers were simply killed. Since this is no longer acceptable, we should not expect the Maori system alone to be able to create ways of dealing with murder and its consequences. Jackson (103) says we should at least try, otherwise we simply perpetuate a monocultural system; the Roper report on prisons agrees (151).

The Jackson report argues that the end, justice, is commonly desired but better and fairer means of reaching it need to be developed. He uses the analogy of kohanga reo, where children are taught concepts to deal with the world while at the same time learning and preserving the language. Those involved believe that they are helping to restore to the people traditional strengths and values.

Courts operated by tribal councils on North American native reservations have been working for years. Maori people have been actively discussing whether similar institutions could be established under iwi authorities. Limited powers to fine or otherwise punish used to exist for marae committees. Jackson goes further than this, but there is no doubt that, within the general law, community involvement is already moving along the path of parallel systems.

However, the then deputy prime minister and minister of justice, Geoffrey Palmer, refused to accept the Jackson report, perhaps thereby confirming that we are still a monocultural country. Government, it seems, will provide funds for Maori language preschools or training programmes, but when it comes to justice there is to be one justice for all – that guaranteed by Article I of the Treaty of Waitangi. What of Article II of the Treaty, which guaranteed Maori rangatiratanga and the right to use their cultural means to achieve their cultural ends?

Article II is not just about forests, fisheries, and other resources; it is about the authority system which protects these taonga or treasures for the people and regulates their use. The Jackson report is calling for the Article I partner to recognise the Article II partner in developing new systems of social control. As Jackson says, the Pakeha system is not working; there is no choice but to allow Maori people the opportunity to see if they can do better; surely they can do no worse (103). Jackson may, of course, be quite wrong. The Pakeha system may well decide that the choice is theirs and that they will not allow provision for this alternative. Prime Minister Palmer said so when the report was presented to Government. It is also, of course, an article of faith on Jackson's part that Maori people can do no worse than the present system and might indeed do better.

The techniques required to make a rapist stop raping, or a wife beater quit, or a bank robber desist, or a child sexual abuser give up still elude the Pakeha justice system and almost certainly require extremely sophisticated understandings of how people get to be this way, and of what must be done if they are to change. The Jackson proposals would need progressive and graduated implementation, development of Maori expertise through their own training programmes, and careful attention to the detail of relating the two systems. Back in the 1950s legal challenges on appeal destroyed the confidence of marae committees in administration of the legal powers they then had. Two systems can operate in parallel but neither must appear to undermine the other. Yet they cannot be separate systems entirely. The tightest and most rigorous sanctions and controls will be needed to keep the offender in place while the processes of change begin to work. What will motivate the alienated Maori to give up the habits of a lifetime? For what gain? And if, behind the distorted behaviour patterns that lead to violence, there are serious psychiatric problems, who will cope with these? None of these are insuperable problems and none are good reasons to reject the possibility of sentencing and rehabilitation based on Maori authority systems. But they call for answers.

There is no ready-made Maori justice system out there waiting to take over from the police, the courts, the probation service, the prisons, and the psychiatric institutions, no culturally explicit set of practices which would constitute an alternative system. But there are broad statements of cultural principle and a basis from which a Maori jurisprudence or philosophy for the practice of justice can be developed. We return to this matter in Chapter 16.

In a multi-cultural society common standards of behaviour form the basis of a common society and from there we can all move towards understanding and accepting differences. All appear to reject violent behaviour but all must change if we are to reduce or eliminate it. Such changes will be different and differently managed according to cultural style and practice.

Monoculturalism is oppressive and is itself violent.

# 9
# Violence and National Identity

National identity consists of the simplified but powerful myths people have about themselves – myths in the sense of truth that is greater than the truth. National identity may be based on what a nation has achieved in its past, as in the case of Athens in the Age of Pericles. It may be about what a nation can achieve now, as in the case of contemporary Japan. But generally it is about character and style.

Pakeha New Zealand has only a shallow history in this country. Some of our myths, for example that Westminster-style democracy achieves equality, derive from the longer past of Britain. And for historical reasons, our politicians have, until recently, tied our economy, our trade, and other aspects of national pride to Britain.

Thus, if there was a war in which Britain was involved, we felt compelled to be there too. But when the United States wished to involve us in their wars in Asia, our politicians became deviously reluctant. Even so, token volunteer forces were sent to Korea and to Vietnam. Not until we banned nuclear ships from our harbours did we appear to strike free from traditional northern hemisphere military ties. Our wish to be part of the movement to rid the world of nuclear weapons, one objective of the peace movement generally, is comparable to the international ban on chemical weapons after World War I which persisted for seventy years. In terms of national identity, we are not anti-war – indeed, in our short history, war has been a fairly regular preoccupation. For a country that has neither land frontiers nor the resources to wage war effectively, we must ask why (175).

The first aggressive acts of our Pakeha ancestors were against the Maori, although right there at the start we tried to get someone else to do the dirty work for us. The British were extremely reluctant to commit troops to fight in New Zealand, having taken a drubbing from the New England states in America sixty years previously and as a result lost out in wealth as well as prestige. The annexation of New Zealand was, indeed, opposed by some precisely because it stretched the thin red line of British military control too far from Whitehall. Supply lines were ludicrously long and costly; the British troops had little notion of living off the land (21, 22). Thus, the earliest military policy for New Zealand was made in Australia, and it was not until 1852 that New Zealand was supposed to have any independent military competence of its own at all. Australian and British colonial troops continued to fight the settlers' wars for them until well into the 1870s. There were Australian troops at Rangiriri in 1862, and this engagement is proudly listed at the Australian National War Memorial Museum as the first overseas war of that country.

The early pioneering enterprise that began with a battle *for* the land was followed by a battle *with* the land. The dominant spirit was one of independence and personal accomplishment through the tough work of clearing the bush by slashing and burning.

Grey and his immediate successors delayed the establishment of provincial government because ·of the distrust and rejection of the settler community. But when it finally happened the distrust was transferred upstairs as the provincials fought bitterly to prevent the establishment of a national administration. There is a deep strand of parochialism here which is strangely at odds with our readiness to shift from place to place.

The pioneering era required a gritty toughness of character (176). Whereas the Maori 'lived light' on the land, the pioneers set out to impose an alien image of pastoral England on the dark, dank bushlands. Through to the present the clearing of land has continued long after it has become obvious that there was no good economic reason to do so. Whacking down the bush became an obsession, scrub-cutting a duty.

We who have inherited this land have also inherited what those pioneers did to it and what it did to them in the process. Although much of it remains beautiful, a great deal has been so scarred that parts may simply become arid deserts, continuing symbols of the violence done to the land.

The New Zealand masculine stereotype has its foundations in this pioneering past. Male 'mateship' was built upon 'slogging it out together', on mutual dependency for long periods of time (174). Often solitary males became migratory, looking for work. They drove the cattle, mustered the high country, migrated with the shearing, explored the hinterland, set up outposts of farm or settlement. Men deprived of the moderating influence of women and families felt the need to be tougher than they really were, and dared not display tenderness to one another, perhaps because of homophobia. Their asexual mateship involved demonstrations of toughness that often become competitive. Woodchopping competitions, sheep-shearing championships, the male skills of fencing and of tug-of-war linger on still. The physical stereotype of the New Zealand male is not necessarily the bulging weight-lifter or the hefty front-row forward but the nimble half-back, the 'wiry little bugger' who can 'hang on in there'. The same applies to his dog. While wild pigs were here from Cook's time, we later introduced game animals for men to kill. A great deal of our national economy involves killing: we are, after all, a nation who built its prosperity on the slaughter of millions of animals each year. Being rough was a sign you could be tough.

Stuck down in the South Pacific twelve thousand miles from our European cultural roots, ultimately we had to depend upon ourselves since we could not bring ourselves to depend upon what the Maori had to offer. To create the settler idyll, planks had to be chipped with adzes from felled timber and houses made from local mud. While the wealthier and the missionaries came with pre-fabricated houses or had them shipped across from Australia, the pioneer settlers made their own. Wooden door bolts were fashioned when no metal hardware was available. Ingenious flumes brought water right to the house. Until corrugated iron arrived, thatching had to be devised. Beds were made from sacking and strips of hide. We had to be inventive with what was here.

To do all this, resourcefulness and ingenuity were needed and came to be highly valued. People who have never touched the stuff still use the image of number 8 fencing wire and its myriad uses as shorthand for New Zealand inventiveness and the infinite capacity to make do. Stick an old coathanger in the radio aerial input on the car. She may not be perfect, mate, but she'll be right.

The theme of the tough, resourceful Kiwi bloke, modest, but capable of anger when roused, and of violence if necessary, recurs throughout our short but surprisingly turbulent history.

While literary pundits may argue as to whether New Zealand literature reflects the national character, the cartoonists, the comedians, and the satirists have no such qualms. They sharpen the stereotype in their portrayal of Barry Crump, Fred Dagg, and Footrot Flats. It is there all right, alive and well in pub-lore and popular culture, and now in TV advertising.

The pioneering era did not come to an end until the nation had a secure political structure. The development of a national transport infrastructure wiped out many regional differences. The export of farm products brought economic security. Then came our first great national demonstration of unity, involvement of New Zealanders in the battlefields of World War I. An extraordinary proportion of young New Zealand men were conscripted to fight. Myths of glory were created to recruit them, to sustain them through incompetently led battles, dreadful fighting conditions, and appalling losses, and to justify these losses to those left behind. Throughout New Zealand every little settlement has its war memorial or memorial hall (132).

The glorification of this dreadful war reached its peak with the Gallipoli campaign (178, 222, 223). This was a terrible defeat, the result of gross military mismanagement, poor information, and official stubbornness. The colonial forces took the brunt in trying to win territory for which there was little strategic justification. The Bosphorous had no military value and even if there had been some strategy to invade Eurasia, this was surely not the place to start. It has taken seventy-five years for the 'glory' of this fiasco to die, and even now it is to 'heroism' that Anzac Day observances are dedicated, not to reminders of the callous waste of the lives of colonial youth for purposes of National Glory. Of course there were objectors to the fighting on grounds of conscience; but we treated them badly – and buried the evidence of ill-treatment (19).

Out of this horror, waste, and carnage came the assertion of nationhood, the name ANZAC, and one of our earliest affiliate ties with Australia. It should have been the point at which we realised that British military authority simply regarded New Zealand soldiers as a commodity. We were used, blatantly and shamelessly. It should have been the point at which, like the Australians, we finally wrenched free into a separate, assertive national identity. Instead, we slipped back into economic and cultural dependence on Britain. But the image of male heroism in violent actions remains. That we are not yet free from this myth is demonstrated by the fact that in 1987 a memorial was built on New Zealand soil to commemorate Kemal Ataturk, the revolutionary leader whose troops destroyed so many of ours at Gallipoli.

The economic depression of the 1930s may well be the forge in which the New Zealand character was annealed. Here we see all the positive strengths – the making do, the resourcefulness, the resilience, the dour stubbornness, the hanging on and getting by. But there were also the domestic upheavals, the marriages that did not survive the brutalising effect that living in the company of men on relief work, making roads, planting forests or just being unemployed, had on many men. When the history of our national character comes to be written, we suspect that for New Zealand it is the 1930s that will reveal the bed-rock.

In World War II a new level of New Zealand identity was constructed, this time, more true to our real selves. Apart from the Maori Battalion, the New Zealand units do not stand out in the battle records of World War II. They did their job in Greece, Crete, North Africa, Italy, and in the Pacific sector. The battle honours they earned tell one story. Off the battlefield our troops developed a reputation for lack of discipline, pillaging, lawlessness, and a kind of wild opportunism, the real history of which is only now being written (237). In this war, too, conscientious objectors and internees in prison camps here were treated harshly (85, 92).

World War II acted as a watershed. It transformed New Zealand into an industrial nation, and began to loosen the economic apron strings which had tied us to Mother England. Britain, in reconstruction, became increasingly involved with Europe, and we were forced, reluctantly and belatedly, to seek other markets and other ties of association.

War is, of course, about winning: And New Zealanders, wherever they are engaged in competition, look for total victory – in war, in sport, in politics, in business. Was it an accident that the highest mountain in the world was conquered by a New Zealander? Is the Americas Cup just another yacht race? And the Whitbread Round the World race – do we own it? The international athletic circuit, and especially the Olympics, have from Lovelock onwards been arenas where our tiny little nation foots it with the high and mighty, and wins, quite disproportionately to our size.

There is one arena where winning is not enough, where we must win all the time, totally, and for ever, and that is on the rugby field. In 1928 the All Black Invincibles set the model by winning every match of their tour. Ever since there has been an obsession with more than winning – with total annihilation: nothing else is good enough! We will discuss this further in Chapter 10.

In other areas, too, aggression is rife. Our driving standards and annual road toll are a national disgrace. The death rate here (3.56 per 10,000 registered vehicles) is higher than in any similar country. (Sweden 2.5, the United States 2.7, Canada 2.8, Britain 3.2, Australia 3.4.) Speed, dangerous passing and generally competitive and aggressive driving have been the subject of official comment, with alcohol as a concomitant factor (153).

In all of this image-making, the national identity is couched in male terms. But some of the most effective demythologised portrayals of the nature of New Zealand have come from literary and artistic works by women. There is no better portrayal of station life than the early account of Lady Barker (15) or Mona Anderson's *A River Rules My Life* (6). Eileen Duggan, Katherine Mansfield, Sylvia Ashton-Warner, Keri Hulme, Renée, Patricia Grace, Fiona Kidman, Sue McCauley, Joy Cowley have all contributed to the composite portrait of who we are. Of our male writers, perhaps John Mulgan's *Man Alone* stands as the prototypic male novel, in its depiction of an ordinary bloke, an outsider who becomes a killer outlaw, runs away into the bush, and is hunted down (159).

Lawless men have became the anti-heroes of our national folklore. Stanley Graham held out against the police in the West Coast bush for many days in 1961 killing both police and neighbours in the process. He was a semi-dazed paranoid isolate, a lonely farmer who, fearing dispossession, was forced into insanity, killed his oppressors, and in doing so became part of our folk-history. George Wilder, the great prison escaper of the early 1960s, seemingly could not be constrained by any authority and enjoyed great public notoriety. This image of the outsider battling authority and, at least for a time, winning, connects powerfully with New Zealand attitudes to authority and the fragile controls that curb male aggression.

As long as New Zealanders fail to see and accept the role which violence plays in our history, our national mythology, and our national identity, we will continue to be victims of ourselves.

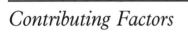

*Contributing Factors*

# 10

# Violence and Sport: Good Clean Fun?

New Zealanders have high participation rates in organised sport. A *Listener* survey listed the registered membership of twenty-two major sports (206). They total over one million participants.

The pattern is gender related. While both sexes have high rates of sporting activity at high school, the traditional female role takes many women away from active sport and onto the sidelines cheering their menfolk or children on, or into the kitchens, the laundry, or the clubrooms, or into the car chauffeuring the children and socialising them into the rules of the game.

What are these rules? Every sport has its own code, but in the predominantly male sports there are rules behind the rules, rules of mateship, rules of honour, rules of toughness, and rules that not only condone but actually encourage violence (11). Dazzling footwork in a rugby player may bring the crowd to its feet with a roar of delight, but the punch up after a ruck will evoke an equal level of vicarious excitement. How safe it is to identify with the aggressor from the security of the stands!

Officials say that they are concerned about sports injuries and modify the rules to protect the players. The only rules they can change are the overt rules, which, although they may seem to limit violence and aggression, do little to change the covert rules. For all this cosmetic activity, and however well-intentioned it may be, sports injuries continue to happen and many are serious. The worst result in spinal injury and even death; but there are many more broken jaws, fractured limbs, deep concussions, broken noses, and thousands of minor injuries such as finger dislocations, minor breaks, and serious abrasions. Quite apart from anything else, the cost during the winter of sports injuries pouring through the accident and emergency departments of hospitals is appalling. In 1988 sports injuries resulted in 31,688 claims to the Accident Compensation Corporation, which paid out over $56 million. Rugby, with one-fifth of the sportspeople, had the greatest number of injury claims (8,726), costing over $16 million, some $5 million more than proportionate. Rugby injuries also cost about 10 per cent more per claim on average (1).

Alcohol abuse costs the country between $690 million and $880 million per year (180). Tobacco costs are higher, at around $1,000 million (248) and traffic accidents probably cost more (152). Together this totals more than 10 per cent of GNP. Sporting costs may seem minor at $56 million but all are costs that might be eliminated.

Seemingly dangerous sports such as hang-gliding, parachute diving or jumping off bridges on the ends of elastic bands result in nothing like the serious consequences of a 'friendly game of rugby'. Why do men put themselves at risk of injury, pain, disfigurement, and physical and mental disability by playing dangerous sports such as boxing and rugby? Surely there are other ways to exercise, to experience companionship, the putative 'high' of the adrenalin rush, the thrill of success, the extension to the limits of one's capacity without the likelihood of serious physical injury to oneself or others.

The value which has come to be placed upon the body contact sports can not be wholly explained in terms of demonstrations of physical prowess. These sports have many of the attributes of a cult or religion (232). The membership is exclusive; there are rituals of entry which involve renunciation of more 'normal' life-styles (no sex before the match, for example); new recruits at initiation are subjected to ordeals of physical endurance; there is worship of ancestral figures, the ritual exchange of totem objects (cups and trophies), badges, uniforms, and other clothing of membership; and, ruling over all, there is the council of elders, one of whom becomes the high priest. The brotherhood extends beyond nations, although nowhere is the ritual game played more competitively than between nations.

The media have played an important role in the development of these phenomena, concentrating as they do upon the sensational action and elevating sporting heroes to star-like status. Every four years the cult reaches near hysterical climax in the Olympic games. The original Olympic games were, indeed, a religious festival, with strong aesthetic value placed on physique and performance rather than competition and records. The Romans took over the concept but debased it into the blood-letting of gladiatorial spectacles. The cult dispersed with the Roman Empire. The modern Olympiad has its rituals which seemingly grow in number with each Olympic games. To the original dedication to the glory of sport has been added the opening and closing ceremonies, the swearing in, the dress conventions, the rituals of competition, the national medal counts, the medal ceremonies, the media spectacles of folk dancing, and now the more sinister rituals of security protection and terrorist threats.

Goldstein believes that sports violence can be viewed in three ways: as an extension of the violence in the rest of society, so that if violence in general escalates then it will also increase in sport; as ritual display where teams and supporters take part in all the rituals surrounding the game, such as drinking before and after the game, chanting and cheering during the game, and the types of clothes worn by the players and their supporters; and as a training ground for masculine role behaviour (81).

Sport plays a substantial, if not a primary, role in the formulation of the male role (216). Those who claim that sport is character forming may well be right. But what are the character attributes so formed? Sports idealogues believe sport encourages discipline, self-esteem, concentration, skill, fitness, courage, stoicism, fortitude, team spirit, loyalty, and unyielding competitiveness (96). But sport also has a hidden agenda, which is to encourage pugnacity, brutality, callous disregard for the effects of one's behaviour on others, ego aggrandizement, and selfishness.

Why is it that our society almost always segregates organised sport on gender lines? There are a few exceptions, such as mixed doubles in tennis, but they are of low status. We should note that the recreations which pit the individual against nature or the elements, such as mountain climbing, hang-gliding, surfing and windsurfing, are enjoyed by both sexes. Yet even these sports segregate the sexes when it comes to competition.

Both in fiction, for example Greg McGee's *Foreskin's Lament* (131), and in works of social commentary, for example Felix Donnelly's *Big Boys Don't Cry* (52) or Jock Phillips' *A Man's Country?* (174) a mirror has been held up so that we can see the grosser aspects of the way in which our society patterns male behaviour. Rugby is just another step in the toughening process whereby men must hide their real humanity, cover up their feelings, and relinquish their sensitivity. The place of 'The Game' in the national psyche has its own literature, reviewed by Geoff Fougere in a brief but sharp article in which he focuses on sport as a unifier of an otherwise divided nation (66). Phillips also explores the same theme writing about rugby, war, nationhood and masculinity (173).

Rugby carries a heavy 'cultural baggage'. In Fougere's phrase, it is a 'white man's game' (119), which though sometimes used to bridge cultural gaps has, in the context of sporting contacts with South Africa, a capacity to create allegiance like no other game. Men are trained not to trust other people – even other men except within the bonded brotherhood of the sporting club, the drinking club, the business club, or the similar arenas where men make deals with other like-minded men and exclude the rest.

This kind of exclusivity creates watertight social compartments. Looking in, there is loyalty, comradeship, and a sense of belonging. Looking out, there is suspicion, distrust, hostility, and aggression.

The whole phenomenon of rugby, not just the game itself, is paradigmatic of the stereotypic male role and character. Of course, not every rugby player is nasty, brutal, and violent. But we are not speaking of individual cases. We are speaking of rugby as a further example of institutions that support, sanction, and perpetuate the expression of violence in our society.

There may be those who think that rugby can somehow be 'cleaned up' or sanitised, but we doubt this. The game is about men who win, and about the forces in our society that give them the drive to win and the right to use physical violence both on and off the field. For everyone who has played rugby the experience of physical violence at close quarters remains an integral part of their total experience. Other sports may become violent but rugby *is* violent – remove the violence and you no longer have the game.

Throughout their lives, those who have played the game and played it well will continue to receive benefits from other members of the rugby tribe. For example, why should two Auckland rugby representatives who harassed two young women be discharged without conviction because 'both had promising rugby careers' (*Waikato Times*, 28 October 1988)? They 'stood a chance to play for New Zealand but would be prevented if convicted' and this would 'put your sporting careers in jeopardy,' the judge said. In an ironic twist, the judge then ordered that they pay $250 each to the St John's Ambulance, the organisation whose job it is, amongst other things, to patch up wounded rugby players!

Rugby prowess will help your career, whether you are a teacher or a member of the Stock Exchange. And should you be an All Black, even if for only one game, the fact will be remembered throughout your life until your obituary is written – and in the case of the great rugby heroes, even beyond.

Intelligent men do play rugby, and manage to stay intelligent. The same cannot be said for boxing. However ancient, and lauded with the rhetoric of noble action, the 'manly art of self-defence' regularly produces a vegetable-like state in its hero-victims. There is a dangerous dynamic at work here. Young men, usually from minority and disadvantaged backgrounds, become lured into a gradual process of physical self-sacrifice, the motive being the lure of celebrity status, the big purse, and the adulation of a small but vocal public.

It is not surprising that a society that will not give up beating its children will not give up a blood sport such as boxing. At the 1988 Olympics in Seoul, the most dismal spectacle was the riot that broke out when the Korean boxing officials disagreed with the referee's decision and proceeded to attack him because the Korean fighter had lost the bout. In the context of the 'sport' of fighting, fighting as an expression of anger broke out as would never be the case in a dispute over a decision in, say, gymnastics.

The boxing ring or the rugby field is a four-sided frame that contains action which we try to divorce from action that occurs outside that frame. To assert that behaviour can be switched on and off in this way implies that the players have almost superhuman powers of dissociation. Boxing celebrities such as Mike Tyson engage in violent behaviour in night-clubs, bedrooms, or almost anywhere that they may be. On occasion rugby players have had to be restrained when they became aggressive after a match, off the field, outside the frame.

Amongst research that we guess will never be done, but which we would like to see done, is an investigation into the correlation between behaviour on the rugby field and domestic violence and child abuse. We do know that rugby players endorse violence as a form of conflict resolution more frequently than those who have not been 'socialised' into the game (187).

The cult of rugby elevates its values into an ideology, and the rules of the game into great moral truths. As the Rugby Anthem (220) 'On the Ball', written in 1887, puts it:

*Remember then boys as you journey through life*
*There's a Goal to be reached bye and bye,*
*And he who runs true why he's bound to get through*
*And perhaps score a Goal for his try*

*This life's but a scrummage we cannot get through*
*But with many a kick and a blow*
*And then in the end though we dodge and defend*
*Still that sure collar 'Death' takes us low. (35)*

The metaphors are so powerful that they eventually become the reality. The language of rugby becomes the language of life, and it is a language of violence. You beat the other side, just as your father beat you. You score as in sexual conquest, and proceed to tell the boys. The team must be whipped into shape so that it can wallop the other side. Next time you hear rugby commentary, listen for the language of violence.

In the sponsorship of sport, the line-up of sponsors and products with gender stereotypes is significant. Who sponsors netball? The manufacturers of yoghurt, a chocolate drink, and women's underwear. Who sponsors women's tennis? A cosmetic company. And who sponsors rugby? The liquor giants.

It is not only the sporting bodies themselves who make money out of sport, but the manufacturers of sporting goods and of the products that are associated with male habits: beer, tobacco, and motoring products. They, and their advertising agencies, all have an obvious interest in increasing patterns of consumption by association with 'macho' male sports.

Commercial companies do not sponsor sporting events out of altruism or for the glory of sport, although this is the impression they give to the young and the naive (190). They do it for dollars – sponsorship is just another name for advertising. This was recognised by the Royal Commission into Broadcasting in 1986 (208). The liquor and tobacco industries have run into opposition in advertising their products in the normal commercial way, and have therefore turned to sponsorship as a way of bending the rules. They, and other groups such as sporting goods manufacturers, know that there is a large, continuous, and captive audience upon whom they can exercise the basic advertising formula that repeated exposure creates a preference. This is even more effective if you can use heroic figures as part of the formula, or even get them to endorse the product.

The sponsorship 'advertisements' make heavy use of both sexual innuendo and images of violence, such as 'Give 'em a taste'. This, at its mildest, might mean a sip of beer, but it has undertones of a mouthful of knuckles or, indeed, of the salt of blood. The slogan has now been adopted by the fans who shout it from the banks when the game has become too tame.

Alternatively, there is the use identification, as though the product were the game and the game were the product. The familiar rugby beer slogan 'We are Rugby', were it applied to 'We are netball' would lose impact not only because it does not rhyme with the product name, but also because no red-blooded male would want to identify with netball, and women are not the major drinkers of beer. Sport makes money for advertisers and violent sport makes more money. No wonder the liquor interests support rugby.

As the male cult of sport has developed and expanded, so other sports previously less locked into the violence syndrome have come to glorify the violent attack which wins the game. Rugby league was never a parlour game, but the personality cult has accentuated the importance of flattening your opponent. The hysteria surrounding rugby league reaches even greater heights when nationalistic and ethnic elements are the feature of the match.

The increasing violence in many sports is reflected in the gear players now wear. Cricketers who used to play that quiet Sunday game on the village green now enter the sporting arena padded and masked like American gridiron footballers. Gridiron footballers themselves look more like robotic androids – you tell them apart only by their numbers. The American football coach of a major Ivy League team once told us that he chose his players for their capacity to tackle calmly and, in cold blood, to stop the opponent dead! He did not want players who were likely to be clouded with anger or hate, but simply machines who would play good football. This is the epitome of dehumanised violence – there is no emotion involved.

What concerns us here is the passive acceptance by large mass audiences of behaviour that would be unacceptable and illegal in another frame. We will see in the next chapter how this same passive spectator quality is induced through the depiction of violence by the media. The spectator is so distanced from the punch, the blood, the crack of the breaking bone, that the mind absorbs only the visual image of the violence and none of the pain or hurt. Once that connection has been snapped, the spectator may become the perpetrator of violence, not thinking of its human consequences but only of the personal need to get rid of frustration, anger, or hate.

Spectators are not always passive and the creeping rot of spectator violence has already reached this country, particularly in the not-infrequent occurrence of post-rugby match fracas and in throwing beer cans when the crowd is angered or bored. One view tended to minimise the riot phenomenon associated with international soccer by making it seem like some territorial ritual display (140). No one should minimise the dangerous nature of mob violence. The riots after games clearly show the error of the catharsis theory: young males are more dangerous *after* watching a violent game than they were before. It also shows the error of those who would claim that sporting contests are a benign substitute for war. They are not a substitute; they *are* war. They have all the characteristics of battles, including the blood, the humiliation of defeat, motives of revenge, and the intoxicating joy of victory.

Even those disposed to peace can find themselves caught up in the behaviour of combat. The most noted example in New Zealand was the mirror image of the behaviour of the riot police and the protestors during the 1981 Springbok tour. Civil servants wore armour, senior executives cut through wire and climbed barricades. While the police escalated their arms and control tactics to the level of a military operation, the legacy for New Zealand society was not only a set of Darth Vader images but also a police capability that will never be eliminated. Within months of the Springbok tour, long batons were being used to empty out a country dance hall, and now traffic officers are also armed with them.

The Springbok tour was the closest that New Zealand has ever come to a state of civil war, and only time will tell how close we came to the declaration of a state of emergency to control civilian protest so that the tour could go on. Night after night, television screens were filled with images that resembled police action in South Africa or Northern Ireland – and all of this was because of a game? Clearly not. One section of New Zealand cared passionately about racial freedom while another cared passionately about rugby and *only* rugby. Nothing else in this country could engender such feelings.

# 11

## Guns:
## The Trigger Pulls The Finger

It is a myth of popular psychology that our actions are initiated by ourselves, that we are fully conscious of and responsible for all that we do and intend. The truth of the matter is that most of our behaviour is going on from moment to moment in response to stimuli of which we are but dimly aware. We cross our legs, shuffle in our chair, touch our chin. Even the activity of reading a book involves stimulus-directed behaviour which we initiate but which then runs on like a railway train until we signal it to stop. Most behaviour is under what psychologists call stimulus control; that is, because of past experience, the appearance, whether conscious or not, of a signal of some sort, whether external or internal to ourselves, brings about a more or less automatic response.

We ought then to attend very closely to the signals that instigate violence. We can never eliminate them entirely, but we should set about limiting, or detoxifying, the sea of stimuli in which we swim. This is an enormous task because, without realising it, we have allowed our social environment to become heavily contaminated with the triggers of violence. Just as we have forced the physical environment to carry many dangers to itself – the depletion of the ozone layer, the increase in gases which produce the 'greenhouse effect', acid rain, the biological death of inland waters, leachates and chemical contaminants – so, too, have we allowed the stimuli to violence to creep into our daily perceptual environment. We attend only to the dramatic, the novel, the ultra-violent in specific incidents which capture our attention.

Images directly linked to sexual bondage and domination are now freely scattered through our visual world. Black leather, metal chains and studs, bonds, thongs and straps, heavy belts and buckles and heavy boots are now fashion items. Have they been 'liberated' from the world of sado-masochism or are we being induced to tolerate it?

We have indicated elsewhere (197) how the language of violence reflects thought patterns of a violent nature. Each year we ask our students to collect examples of such phrases as 'it suddenly hit me', 'I was struck by', 'beating around the bush', 'crack the whip', 'punch home a point', 'thrash out a solution', and so on. Such violent expressions reflect the latent acceptance of violent phenomena. We litter ordinary life with the verbal spice of sanctioned violence.

We will later discuss bad habits of stress management, poor frustration controls, and other components of the formula that lies behind an overt violent act. In this chapter we will focus on the more flagrant stimuli to violence, the most dramatic example of which is euphemistically referred to as the firearms question. Who should be licensed to have guns, for what purposes, and how can their presence in the social environment be limited and controlled to prevent antisocial and illegitimate use?

Here we can report on a small but fascinating literature which has attempted to address the question: does the finger pull the trigger or the trigger pull the finger (26, 251)? In one study, the ingenious researchers used the amount of honking of the car horn at a flatbed truck stalled at traffic lights as a measure of aggression. Honking at a source of annoyance and frustration may not seem very violent, and normally it is not; however, the experiment compared two situations: honking when the back of the truck was empty, and honking when guns were clearly visible on the back of the truck. There was more honking at the truck carrying guns than at the empty one. The stimulus of the guns increased the likelihood that the hand would hit the horn (25).

There is not much research on how the state of the watcher affects the action, but such evidence as we do have indicates that the more aroused the person, the greater the likelihood that the presentation of violent stimuli will be followed by violent action (25).

Although the law permits a person to use reasonable force in self-defence, there are many ways, other than the use of firearms, to defend oneself from possible harm. Jimmy Raupata, an unarmed burglar, was shot dead in 1989 by Mark Williams, a gun collector. If Mark Williams had not had ready access to a gun, and had picked up a tennis racket when he went to investigate the noise in a nearby flat, Jimmy Raupata, thirty-four years old, father of five, would not have lost his life. Williams was not charged with murder or even manslaughter.

It must be obvious that the more guns there are available in society, the more often they will be used aggressively. The logical question to ask is therefore: why are guns available at all? In the United States the answer offered by the powerful gun lobby, the National Rifleman's Association, is that the right to bear arms is guaranteed by the constitution and that so-called recreational use of firearms to kill animals is an innocuous activity that should not be inhibited by law (260). These arguments are used by the gun lobby to oppose any restrictions on the owning of firearms.

In New Zealand there is no constitutional protection of the right to own and use guns. But a substantial number of the population – 334,400 individuals – own one million of them. Presumably they do so to shoot ducks, deer, and pigs, but occasionally, they shoot one another (127). In one of our studies, nearly two-thirds of the men studied had, at some time in their lives, been on a hunting expedition (202). We should, therefore, not be surprised when shotgun barrels are shortened and used in armed robberies or to intimidate or force access. Next to knives or bits of wood, they are the most common kind of weapon used. In one-third of the homicides analysed by Gavin Hancock in the *New Zealand Herald* (14 January 1989) guns were the murder weapon.

Many people, including the police, continue to be very concerned about the ease with which firearms are acquired. The man who keeps his gun in a locked cupboard and the bolt elsewhere is a different type of person from the man who takes his gun out and oils, polishes, fondles and flourishes it every night. The frequency of 'accidents' is itself alarming and, while they may not involve malicious intent, they do indicate that a life-threatening instrument is being treated carelessly and casually. Our society tends to glorify the gun and give it a powerful stimulus value. We do this not only by continuing to tell tales of heroism and warfare but by glorifying the violent characteristics of movie and television heroes such as Rambo and by allowing children (usually male) to play with realistic imitations.

This programme of conditioning leads to a denial of what guns really are – instruments with no other purpose than to kill, injure, or intimidate. The marketing of war toys, both those of devastating realism and those that go well beyond into the realms of fantasy, enormously extends the gun as a symbol of violent potential.

The toy industry, of course, denies the truth of such a statement and produces a range of justifications. These include the incorrect notion that imaginative war play is cathartic, and therefore healthy, and that children will use sticks or other makeshift objects in place of guns (250). The real issue is that the market and the manufacturers are locked in a deadly liaison. People buy what the manufacturers offer, especially if it is marketed to produce consumer demand from children, through television advertising, product tie-ins with movies or television programmes, and other exploitative marketing methods. Violence sells, even to little children. There are no more ethics in the toy gun industry than there are in its big brother – the arms industry itself. There is, however, an anti war toy movement in New Zealand called Play for Life arising from concerned women in the preschool movement. In response to it, the government set up a working party in 1989, dominated, however, by toy marketing interests. Further pressure will be needed.

New Zealand does not have a munitions industry and it should, therefore, be quite easy to control the entry of firearms into the country. Customs inspectors are alert to this and we believe them to be vigilant. The slippage occurs when legal imports are used illegally or modified. We wonder, however, why anti-personnel guns such as hand guns or rapid repeater rifles should be licenced for import at all.

Measures to tighten gun ownership by licensing the person rather than the weapon have not been conspicuously successful. Those who possess firearms for illegal use are not likely to have respect for the licensing system. A licensing system will not operate adequately unless there is an adequate reporting or inspection system to ensure that firearms are dismantled and locked away in safety, and that they remain in the possession of the legitimate owner. All this is difficult, but that is no reason to avoid the issues.

The notion that a man is more of a man if he goes hunting, shooting, and fishing may seem anachronistic, if not slightly ridiculous in these urban times, but its romantic force lies at the heart of our inability to eliminate the use of firearms. If we could reduce the need for men to demonstrate sporting prowess by using guns, there would be fewer guns available to fall into the hands of those with criminal intent even if they might seek to acquire them in other ways. What men get from these pastimes – mateship, the development of skill, and outdoor and country experience – they could surely get in other ways. Do you have to kill animals to enjoy fresh air and companionship? If shops sold wild duck, venison, and wild pork, hunters could be licensed and an industry developed, but the hunting and acclimatisation lobby has firmly resisted this, in order to protect the recreational values and the game upon which they depend. The shooting of 'game' is an unequal contest and not, in fact, a game.

Control of guns held by criminals or the potentially criminal is a matter of significant concern to the police, who not only have the responsibility to protect the public but are, themselves, in constant and growing danger. We know from overseas experience that arming the police or worse still, arming the populace, dangerously and disastrously escalates the phenomenon of the trigger pulling the finger. We do not know how close we may have come to accepting this alternative during the 1981 Springbok tour. The problem is to provide the police with adequate means of defense. From time to time there are political appeals for greater arming of the police, not only with firearms but also with tear gas, rubber bullets, and mace. The police have not, to their credit, succumbed to the temptation to argue for this even though the Police Association has begun to argue for arming the force.

But if, as we have shown, guns are such a powerful stimulus to violence, why is not everyone shooting everyone else? The answer is, of course, that most people have learned to control their anger and to resolve conflict non-violently, and so have no use for guns in their lives. But not everyone has such control, and our gun laws allow a very high degree of access to temptation to the most susceptible amongst us.

The military go to extraordinary lengths to implant in the minds of their people proper attitudes towards firearms. The discipline is drilled, the responsibility is deeply impressed on the new recruit, and the authority to issue and to use is severely restricted. Even in times of war, no one may fire until ordered to do so. In the same way, the police do not provide their force with unlimited access to weaponry but restrict it to carefully selected, highly trained, and tightly controlled units. Compare that with the welter of slaughter toys bought and delivered into the hands of the young every Christmas, or an average night's fare on television, and you will see the contrast between control and mayhem.

War, and the glory of war, played a greater and more jingoistic role in the founding of Australian identity than might seem the case in New Zealand. But the effect here was just as significant, indeed profound. We found ourselves at war; we 'came of age' through war. Nothing speaks so strongly of the ideology of violence in our culture than this fact.

New Zealand does not actually have a glorious tradition of military victory and conquest whatever the popular mythology may say. When it comes to warfare we are not actually very good. The early wars against the Maori produced neither victories nor heroes. On the part of the colonial troops there was an appalling display of disorder, indiscipline, defeat or near defeat, and inability to adapt to a new environment, a new adversary, and a new style of warfare. It was not the performance of the colonial troops that came to be studied at Sandhurst; it was the strategies of the Waikato warriors in the Waikato campaign and of Titokowaru in Taranaki.

After that we joined in other people's wars as extra troops for causes that were as remote as the battlefields. Nevertheless, jingoism whipped up a sense of patriotic pride strong enough to bring young men to the point where they were prepared to kill, to be killed or to be maimed. The military cult ensured that the horrors of war were more than balanced by the glories of war.

The military themselves claim that they are merely an instrument to serve social and political ends, that they hate war and that, like the American football coach we quoted earlier, they want no truck with those who are out for blood and guts. To train people to suppress emotions such as fear requires the development of strong internal control. The military, however, have always considered this inadequate, so soldiers operate under strict lines of command and the command itself is ultimately under civilian political control.

Even under the strictest conditions of external control, many men still have a problem in controlling negative feelings. Many 'stiff upper lip' men may break out when temporarily away from external controls either at home or abroad. The same problems with control are obvious in civil protests such as those during the Springbok tour. The dam breaks very easily.

The relative infrequency of public disorder is not evidence of lack of inclination but of the ubiquity and strength of the controls that ordinarily apply. We are not a pacifist or peaceable people. We are controlled, and we admire the controller. The strong-minded, strong-armed politician in New Zealand will always climb high in the polls, the more so if he comes across in Parliament like a pugnacious street-fighter or a stern father figure.

Militarism is not publicly pervasive in New Zealand and the military themselves seek to emphasise their public service role in peace-keeping activities, civil defence and such. But beyond the military there exist many quasi-military elements which confirm the authority of force, and reflect the control that structures New Zealand social life and attitudes. Some are obvious, such as the returned servicemen's lobbies, the glorification of military precision displayed by marching girls and brass bands, the re-emergence of military training in schools and proto-military youth and correctional organisations, political endorsement of the 'short sharp shock' punishment for young criminals, and the organisations of the extreme political right.

There are many more triggers than those attached to guns. Some kinds of car scream 'avoid me or watch out'. Some sorts of clothes say 'watch out, I'm dangerous'. A whole fashion style worn by men and by women idealises hardness, harshness, heaviness, and aggressiveness.

All of these become part of a range of stimuli which sustain and often provoke violence. They are signs of our tolerance of the subculture of violence, of a belief system that fixes our fascinated gaze on the face of violence which is, in the end, our own.

# 12

## Sex and Violence

Nowhere in the mythology of violence are there stronger associations nor more powerful images than in the area of sexual behaviour. Sex is commonly regarded as one of the animal urges, its origins atavistic, and its expression instinctive. The reproductive urge is seen as irresistible, the behaviours it engenders believed to be inherently irrational and brutish. These images are heavily patterned by cultural assumptions about human nature, and male nature in particular, and by the way we pattern sexual functioning.

As we saw earlier (Chapters 2 and 3), there is very little behaviour that is pre-programmed or instinctive. Particular kinds of physical and non-physical stimulation are necessary for sexual arousal, including visual, aural, and emotional triggers, although there can be few individuals who can achieve orgasm by conscious thought alone. Were we just biological beings we would need to spend no more than an occasional three to five minutes a time in sexual activity to ensure species continuance and then get on with other things. Culturally learnt behaviour can enhance or inhibit the basic physical processes involved. Sexual behaviour in humans is so free from instinctive patterning that it is totally under psychological control, although unconscious mechanisms may interfere with conscious intentions. The biochemical and physiological patterns associated with sexual arousal and performance are wide open for cultural patterning from that early moment in life when the midwife pronounces the gender of the new-born infant.

Thereafter, in subtle and not-so-subtle ways, the sexual stereotyping of the child will be differentiated by naming, by labelling, by selective attention to any behaviour that might carry a sexual connotation, such as rubbing, grooming, touching, covering, modesty, and display, so that sexual identity is socially and culturally fixed by the second year (155).

One of the widest cross-cultural studies of sexual behaviour ever undertaken (64) demonstrates that whatever human beings are sexually capable of, they do, to some degree or other, in every culture that ever was. Yet the same study shows that every culture establishes norms, very strict rules of sexual preference and performance. Take, for example, the male-defined attributes of female sexual beauty. In our society there are two stereotypes: the slender, sylph-like, tall (but not too tall) woman with big breasts, who is supposed to respond readily and resonantly to the power of male sexuality; and the enveloping, ample, well-rounded figure with large thighs, who is warm, soothing, and motherly (205). When men are sending preferential signals for both of these stereotypes at the same time, it is no wonder that women become confused about what men want. Compare, for example, the depiction of skinny women in *More* magazine with the way that women are portrayed in *Playboy*, or in even more specialised sexual magazines such as *Buff* where grossly obese women are displayed as sexually provocative.

Ford and Beach show that every sexual attribute valued in one culture will be either of little consequence or rejected in another (64). In one society buttocks are valued; in another, large hips or distended ear lobes are highly prized. Frequently, the desired physical attribute is further enhanced by decoration, colouring, or display. In some cultures there is mutilation, or a total cover-up designed to protect women, but which may inflame male fantasies. Note, for example, the way in which nuns are used in pornography. The provocativeness of cover-up is simply the mirror-image of strip-tease.

Anything can be loaded with sexual significance. Take, for example, the fad for discovering phallic symbols everywhere that followed the popular dissemination of Freud's *The Psychopathology of Everyday Life* (68), or the sexual significance now attributed to metal-studded dog collars worn by skinny women in black leather, and now a fashion item all the way from punk rockers to *haute couture*.

If sexuality is so wide a canvas, it is not surprising that projected upon it one sees the full array of cultural phenomena, including those associated with violence. Even before courtship begins, males have learned to display the behaviours that link sex with aggression. Playground dominance is one such example; by teasing and being nasty to the girls, boys attempt to instil patterns of passive submission in their female playmates. Boys can whip their own shirts off, wear skimpy sporting pants, and go almost totally naked at the beach while for girls cover-up has long since begun. These elements of male display and dominance develop into male sexual permissions which sustain the sexual oppression of women. Wearing skimpy beach clothes is not, itself, violent (after all, some women do this too) but it is from such minor components that the patterning of male sexual opportunism can develop. Lots of behaviour, not in and of itself violent, is locked into the pattern of that which is or may become so.

The puberty rites of the Western world continue to promote the image of the sexually predatory male. Belt-notching, 'scoring' a virgin, leaving tell-tale marks such as love bites, using force to obtain submission are all more or less common. Refusal to use condoms or 'riding bareback' and the whole imagery of sexual performance as an equestrian 'stud' experience, for the male are all within the range of normal fantasies and images.

Most men will outgrow these patterns and enter sexual maturity in relationships of equality and mutuality with their partners. But a sizeable number do not, and either remain caught up in immaturity or develop adult patterns of sexual exploitation in which violence becomes an essential component of their sexual performance.

The New Zealand pattern of sexuality has yet to find its Kinsey (113, 114). When it does, the association between sex and violence will be an important and distressing chapter. It has its historical roots in our colonial past. In pioneering days there were few Pakeha women, and sexual exploitation of Maori women by Pakeha men was rampant, as was the indiscriminate spreading of sexual diseases. The demographic records of any Maori locality close to early gold-mining areas, whaling ports, or military barracks reveal a high frequency of infertile women through gonorrheal infection (182).

Not all these liaisons were violent, but frontier societies were characterised by exploitative male behaviour and drunkenness. Men had to be tough, and they were rough on 'their' women. Abandonment was more than just common, it was endemic.

The contemporary link between sex and violence begins with early experience, proceeds through familial culture, and is reinforced by the media and the institutional frameworks already discussed, especially in peer settings in and out of school.

The first association arises when someone who loves you hits you, especially in an erotic area such as the buttocks. How curious it is that a parent, who would never smack a boy on his genitals, will smack him in his anal area. All prospective parents should have explained to them the neurological connections between the anal and the genital areas; all they need to do is constrict their anal sphincter and they will realise the connection. Each time a child is smacked on the bottom, the stimulus he or she receives is sexual and painful at one and the same time. As a general rule, we would say do not strike your child anywhere at all. You are not only modelling a violent form of human interaction and conflict resolution, but you import power into what ought to be a relationship of love. You are also teaching your child that, if the one who loves you hits you, you may then hit the one you love. To use a sexually erogenous zone as the target area for corporal punishment is more perverted and potentially perverting than most people realise (197).

No wonder there has developed an Anglo-Saxon tradition of sexual perversion using canes and whips, stocks and chains, the garb of magistrates, torturers, schoolmasters, military authority, and equestrians. All of this occurs in New Zealand. The extreme phenomena of sado-masochism are disturbing (even if what consenting adults do in private must be their own affair). The marketing and merchandising associated with such perversions is a bizarre flip side of the bland and 'normal' world.

A feminist distinction is useful here. Erotica, which may range all the way from classical literature to masturbatory handbooks, generally depicts mutually enjoyed sexual behaviour between consenting equals. Pornography, on the other hand, is characterised by unequal power relationships between the sexes and therefore by exploitation of women (234). A very high percentage of pornography involves violence with women being bound, beaten, and raped, because that is how sexual power relationships come to be expressed.

Now if pornography stayed on video, within the pages of a book, in the auto-erotic fantasies of men, or in bondage and discipline parlours or brothels, that would be no one else's business. But this is not the case. The research record shows that some men who indulge in pornography try to induce their partners to perform degrading acts (211). The fictions of the pornographic media spill out onto the streets with the voyeurs who are aroused by such stimuli.

It is no coincidence that at a time of increasing awareness of the link between sex and violence there is an unprecedented flood of pornographic material of every kind. Judith Bat-Aba argues that this is a direct response to criticism from the women's movement (124). Pornography exposes a blatant political message, namely, that women must be available to service whatever male sexual need there may be. The voyeur of pornography controls the sexual object depicted, an object which has no human rights and is merely something to be used. Pornography reasserts male control over female sexual objects and is thus, Aba claims, a political response to the feminist rejection of object status.

Rape fantasies, which are widespread in Western culture (95), are confirmed and supported in pornographic material. Over half the male students in a experimental study found a rape story to be sexually arousing, believed that the victim actually enjoyed the rape, and said that they might try to do it themselves if they were assured that they would not be caught (137). Rape in our society will not be eliminated unless pornography as an institutional support is also eliminated (116).

The problem is, of course, how this can be achieved without resort to censorship and bans which not only violate civil rights but also risk creating an underground market and production system. This exists anyway now, here in New Zealand, in video do-it-yourself pornography and very efficient illicit copying and distribution systems. The only final answer is to reduce the needs of those who feel compelled to use pornography as well as keeping up sanctions against those who market it.

It is important to realise that a taste for sex with a dash of violence is not a necessary part of the developmental sequence. It is *always* learned. It can, therefore, be unlearned if we can create the right opportunity and if the person is motivated to change. But it need not be learned at all, and we therefore need very precise and detailed research on how people become so entrapped in pornography that it becomes a necessary part of their sexual life.

Now that we know the importance of the distinction between pornography and erotica, we should also be explaining it to those who are beginning their development towards sexual adulthood (189). Those who would ban such topics from intermediate and high schools are helping to perpetuate the association between sex and violence. Young people, at these ages, are intensely interested in sex in all its varieties and manifestations, and it behoves us to assist them towards a healthy sexuality rather than to rely on traditional taboos. We owe it to young people to separate their experience of sex from the dark shadows and overtones of violence. We should tell them that help is available for those whose sexuality has become contaminated with violent practice. They should not have to bottle up rape fantasies until they are driven to carrying them out in reality. The sexual behaviour clinic is at least as necessary in our society as the clinics which cater for venereal disease or alcoholism.

For as long as there has been commerce there has been the realisation that sex sells. Only recently has come the secondary realisation that the portrayal of violence captures attention and assists in the marketing of sexual merchandise. The exploitation of sex plus violence within the pornography industry has expanded rapidly in the last two decades and, unless checked, could spread and destroy patterns of normal, healthy sexuality.

We know that pornography is a worldwide industry that earns at least $8 billion a year in the United States alone (123). It has become salaciously titillating and daring to import such merchandise into established male coteries such as sporting clubs, bars and drinking places, and executive celebrations. Video porn is now purveyed directly in motels and, indeed, into suburban living-rooms. No longer can we dismiss the depiction of perversion as a matter of personal taste. It has become an economic matter in which the porn industry will create as large a mass market as it can. The market researchers will tell the pornography peddlers where to go to sell their wares. Until now, the market has been male and predominantly middle-aged. Watch now, as the marketeers target the liberated woman, the high-spending young, and the yuppie brigade, until there is designer pornography for every taste and every age, freely available in our wide open, free-market society.

The pornography industry will not control itself because it has no interest in doing so. Neither can we insulate ourselves against the international purveyors of such material. We must therefore begin at the beginning, and raise a generation of New Zealanders who will realise how far that vital taonga, their sexuality, is being exploited for commercial gain by those who accept no responsibility for the consequences of their trade.

The educative alternative seems to us the most practical way to go. The days of effective censorship are over. Modern communications have made it possible to send pornography by fax, and plastic card 'dial a porn' services are beyond censorship. The amateur video camera now puts the production of pornography into the 'do-it-yourself' category. In one major New Zealand town an enterprising private video company will come and film whatever you want, with whoever you want, for a price, and provided you make the arrangements. While all such 'services' may be designed merely to facilitate fantasies, who knows how many men take these fantasies out onto the streets, or into the bedrooms of their partners.

Anti-pornography is one of those strange movements that transcends social categories. Feminists are opposed to pornography, even though there is debate about how to combat it. Some favour censorship (257); others do not (215, 249). The debate unfortunately seems to oppose general civil rights and women's rights. Catharine MacKinnon and Andrea Dworkin regard pornography as a form of sex discrimination and believe that women should be able to claim damages against the producers of pornography for the harm it does to them (10).

The right-wing moralists and religious fundamentalists are also against it, although they favour total censorship without any educational component. Christian moderates are opposed to pornography and favour sex education. The women and men who run preschools are part of the anti-pornography consensus. There was a submission to the Committee of Inquiry into Pornography from three law lecturers who claimed that pornography offended the principles of 'harmony, good-will and fulfilment . . . values enshrined in the Treaty of Waitangi' (*New Zealand Herald*, 16 September 1988).

The very high quality of recent government papers on justice and violence is sustained in the 1989 report on pornography (149). It has an excellent discussion of the nature and impact of pornography, of current views and the situation and a whole section on what might be done about it, with more than 200 recommendations. Since women are the objects in most pornography and men its main consumer (16) it is encouraging to see in this report a clear female perspective.

Many of the specific recommendations call for legal or other control measures. Others reflect on background factors that relate to violence more generally, such as direct media awareness training in schools or support for organisations working to reduce family or sexual violence.

The public have been well served in the way this report covers the field and applies itself to remedies. Many will read and study it but there is really no department of state charged with responsibility to follow it through.

Against the anti-pornography consensus are those who believe that adults should be free to choose for themselves whatever they read or view. As we have shown, that privilege is purchased only at enormous and increasing cost to the sexual safety and security of others, especially of the actors and models used and abused. How free is choice if consumers of pornography have been commercially manipulated? Not all freedoms are equally defensible, and not all freedoms are in fact free. Even at the smorgasbord of pornography, there is no free lunch.

# 13

## Media

Who decided that television programmes should so often feature gun fights, fist fights, motor vehicles used as lethal projectiles, and all the other mayhem that floods the airwaves night after night? Who decided that this was entertainment?

The first answer is, of course, no one person. The second might be the industry. But the third by default and acceptance, is each of us. Through television and video we allow into our living rooms all kinds of people, actions and lifestyles that we would never tolerate in real life. We have allowed television to become the dominant medium for entertainment and information. We have allowed it to grow almost entirely without self-critical awareness and evaluation. The only regular television programme of media comment, *Fourth Estate*, although established for fourteen years, was cancelled late in 1988, to be replaced (and then only briefly) by a media-magazine programme far less trenchant.

Television now rolls on under its own rating-driven impetus and with its own market momentum, becoming more and more the prisoner of its own values. Advisory committees have been swept aside in the process of corporatisation; 'market forces' will now prevail out there in the amoral world of selling; 'If someone will buy it, let's do it; if more people buy it let's do it even more'. Apart from a few public service spots, showing warnings about AIDS or a former All Black captain earnestly urging ordinary blokes to be less violent, television mainly portrays images of mendacity, self-interest, egocentricism, greed, avarice, sex, nationalistic chauvinism, and violence. Or else it shows somewhat peculiar families solving problems of appalling complexity in the space of less than half an hour. But it is television's reinforcement of violence as a way of solving human conflicts that is our present concern.

In two reports, the Mental Health Foundation (89, 144) focused upon television violence, reaching conclusions substantially the same as those of the Surgeon General of the United States in his 1972 report (240). We shall review some of the component research in this chapter. There is no doubt now that television violence initiates violent behaviour in susceptible individuals.

Children's attitudes towards violence and the existence of it in our society are heavily patterned by their television viewing. There is clear evidence that children become desensitised to television violence. There is convincing evidence that television induces children (and probably others too) to view the world as a dangerous and scary place (227). There is also strong evidence that sensational violence is addictive, and that those who succumb move on to a heavy diet of video violence and pornography (144).

Liebert believes that television violence affects all children, not just those 'predisposed to aggression' (128). But the United States Surgeon General's report placed the emphasis on the susceptible audience. Liebert's claim is probably more relevant to the desensitising effect of television violence, rather than to its consequences in violent behaviour, acting out, modelling or copy-cat crime. Clearly, not every male will be aroused by television violence, but the research evidence shows greater susceptibility in boys and young men, and more in some than others. The boys who are most susceptible are likely to watch more television and thus be more exposed to television violence. Already aggressive children are more seriously affected. The cycle escalates. The rest of the audience may believe that what they can withstand (or even enjoy), others can watch with impunity also. This is *simply not true*.

This evidence is overwhelming. The industry is contributing in a major and irresponsible way to the load of violent and criminal behaviour that our society must carry. When we realised that opium was dangerous, we outlawed it, even though it was not dangerous to all who used it. When we realised that cigarette smoking could kill, we warned people of its dangers and have now moved to outlaw advertising and sports sponsorship by tobacco companies.

We are in precisely the same situation with television. Just as the only people who now deny the links between smoking and lung cancer are the tobacco company executives and medical people in their pay, the only people to deny the link between television violence and social violence are television executives and their marketing people. Television personnel even refuse to acknowledge the existence of violence on television by using euphemisms such as 'hard action' programmes

Eron's early work (58) on television violence, aggression, and parent child interaction demonstrated the circular process at work. From his sample group he showed that aggressive children acted violently to their peers and tried to push them round. Eron called it coercive interaction. Peers responded violently. This unpopularity resulted in a poor self-image; poor social adjustment led to poor school performance. Low achievement is punished in our society, so aggressive children, isolated from their peers, do not engage in study or other productive activity, but spend their time watching television and come to believe that the violent situations that they see there may well be a model for them to operate on in the real world. We have known all this for at least a decade, during which the apologists for television violence have, if anything, gained rather than lost ground.

Eron followed the same sample group for years. At the age of twenty-five, the television violence addicts in his sample were more likely to hit their own children than were a control group who had been exposed to less television (100).

The effects of television violence depend on with whom the viewer identifies. Although right may triumph in the intended story-line, the viewer may identify with the wrongdoer's feelings of humiliation, defeat, and powerlessness which seem similar to his or her own.

Belson lists the situations in which violence is more likely to have an effect upon the behaviour of the viewer:

1. *Programmes where violence of a nasty kind appears to be sanctioned by showing it being done in a good cause or with seeming legality . . . This point should be linked up with the finding of a strong tendency by boys to regard their own violent acts (and those of others) as somehow not violent if those acts were 'justified'.*

2. *Programmes that make it easy for boys to identify with the person or persons being violent.*

3. *Programmes where the subject matter is of a kind which tends to demand that the constituent violence be on a large scale, possibly with mass killings. Westerns have tended to be of this kind, as have many programmes (usually films) of the 'epic' variety.*

4. *Programmes where the law enforcer, in order to defeat the villains, does himself commit considerable violence, perhaps of a kind that is tougher and nastier than that used by the villains.*

5. *Programmes in which violence is presented in a context where personal relationships are a major theme. In real life, priority has*

*been given, through training and sanctions, to the protection of our working relationships with other people against the outbreak of serious violence. Presumably the presentation by television of nastiness and violence as a normal element in such relationships tends to reduce in boys such barriers as society has built up in them against being seriously violent in the personal relations context.*

6. *Programmes where violent television of a serious kind is taken out of its developmental context, as when it is just 'thrown in' (i) so that it can be made more violent than its developmental background would warrant it being and (ii) so that boys are not in a position to regard that developmental background as unlikely to apply to them.*

7. *Programmes where the violence is presented with such realism that it is unlikely to be rejected as mere fiction, but instead is given the weight of believability and normality.*

Programme features less likely to stimulate serious violence in boys were:

1. *Programmes where the violence shown is obviously far beyond the capabilities and/or the opportunities of the viewer, as are many forms of science fiction and cartoon programmes.*

2. *Programmes where the violence shown is so ridiculous or far-fetched that it is passed off by boys as having nothing to do with real life.*

3. *Where the programme is humorous in that a humorous presentation or theme is likely to make it harder for the programmer to introduce into it really nasty violence. This is not the same thing as saying that a humorous context somehow lessens the effects of such violence as is inherent in it.*

4. *Programmes where the violence presented is of the purely verbal kind rather than being all or partly of the physical kind. Such programmes are less likely to stimulate serious violence. (At the same time, the evidence indicates that they do produce violence of the* less serious *kind, particularly swearing and the use of bad language).*

5. *Programmes where the television experience leaves the boy satisfied and good tempered – as distinct from tense or irritated or bored.*

6. *Actuality programmes where the televised violence is, as it were,*

> *closely contained within a special environment – as for the*
> *sporting event where the televised violence is in fact an accurate*
> *representation of the specialised violence that is intrinsic to that*
> *particular sport.*
>
> 7. *Programmes where the process of watching a televised event is*
>    *likely to keep boys out of a situation in which violence is likely to*
>    *occur (for example, a televised soccer match).*
>
> 8. *In actuality broadcasting, provided it is not markedly selective and*
>    *is not edited to highlight its more violent elements (23 pp. 18–19).*

In real life, people often seek to minimise their violent acts by explaining that their motives are worthy and the consequences benign. So too may viewers claim that the violent acts on television were justified. Programmes frequently encourage such rationalisation.

Viewing fictionalised violence and watching the real-life violence of the news are very different. Generally the news avoids dwelling too long and too hard on the detail of violence, and when it does move in too close on the blood and gore of the traffic accident, or the shopping centre killing, or the shooting of hostages in the Middle East, the public reaction is one of horror and distaste. On the news you are left in no doubt about the real horror of the event. Bruises don't wipe off with the grease paint. Those who are shot do not appear in next week's episode.

News watching is also less compulsive (even though it is one of the most popular programmes) because you can select from the various items those which interest you. The viewer's attention thus comes and goes, even though the channel does not change. The news is, therefore, generally less likely than fictionalised violence to be harmful (23).

There is one exception, and that is news programmes or documentaries which display crime capsules that might lead to copy-cat crime. We suspect that programmes such as *Crime Watch* may occasionally do this. And we could well imagine that this programme has become obligatory watching for criminals.

The sanitised, trivialised, ritualised act of violence without the consequences which has become the standard model in television cannot be discounted because it lacks realism. What it does is to normalise violence, to make it acceptable, and to act as the trigger or stimulus for some viewers to go out into the real world and to act out the the box's messages that it is O.K. to threaten, coerce, and beat your way to a solution of your problems, whether they are problems of poverty, of sexual inadequacy, of hate, anger or frustration.

The advent of television swept over us when we had no way of knowing what its psychological and social effects were likely to be. There was no previous experience that could guide us – not even the movies. We were not similarly ignorant when video recorders arrived, yet we allowed the video industry to become established before we initiated an adequate set of controls.

In 1984 we attended a conference of researchers on media effects at Yale University. Most of the time was spent on the effects of television, even though the marketing of pornographic and violent videos had become a matter of raging debate throughout the Western world. The video industry has not itself funded research in the matter and all that has happened in New Zealand is a rather ineffectual attempt to classify rental videos.

Such classification simply directs the violence addicts more quickly to the places and shelves where they will find their 'fix', and does nothing at all to control the audience slippage that occurs when those other than the hirer view the video. Suddenly New Zealand children have become exposed to some rather nasty and pernicious material. We never prepared them for this, and still don't seem to want to. We just hope that they won't see what the adults are watching. But they will. For example, the car trashing and other violent scenes in *Mad Max* have led it to receive a classification of 'R18: Contains Violence'. But in both Australian research on video watching (44) and in a New Zealand study (90), children under twelve not only watched this video but rated it amongst their favourites, just behind *Class of 84* which is frequently cited as one of the heaviest sex-and-violence movies available. The Australian and the New Zealand studies both reveal common top-ten favourites, including *They Call Me Bruce* (R16), *Shogun Assassin* (R18), *Ten Tigers of Shaolin* (R16), *Enter the Ninja* (R16), *Bronx Warriors* (R13), *Class of 84* (R20), *Blue Thunder* (R13), *Blade Runner* (R13), *Zapped* (R16), *Lone Wolf McQuade* (R16), *Conan the Barbarian* (R16), *Piranha 2* (R16), *Mad Max* (R18) and *Stir Crazy* (R16). Video recorders are not yet as common as television sets but most children have access to one. Both studies note that video watching is added on to an already heavy diet of television watching.

In a small, previously unpublished Hamilton study of 120 respondents in 1986 we found that 40 per cent of video customers preferred and hired tapes that were classified as containing violence. Women showed a higher preference for comedy and drama, but men preferred 'hard action'. Children encountered age-inappropriate videos in a variety of contexts. They did not usually choose them themselves. Video shops reported that children were sent to choose tapes for adults, or said that they were, and seemed to know where the hard-core videos were located.

The Australian study lists an appalling catalogue of events which children have watched on video and remember (44). The author speaks of the children's 'unwanted memories, from which they cannot free themselves'. These include incidents of mutilation, dismemberment, cannibalism, attack by animals and insects, as well as dramatic violence of a 'domestic' kind. Do we really want children left with memories of violent vomiting, decaying corpses arising from the grave, of people being taken over or possessed by alien malevolent spirits, and being impressed to such a degree that they cannot shake off these memories?

We should stop fooling ourselves when we describe some material as 'adult'. Unless we accept Patricia Bartlett's suggestion to the Committee of Inquiry into Pornography (149) that only videos with a G certificate should be rented or sold, and that those who wish to watch sex and violence should have to go to special age-segregated cinemas to do so, we are left with a dilemma. Shakespeare contains sex and violence. The Roper report on violence could do nothing more on the subject of violent videos than to recommend that they be adequately labelled (150). Our own view is that the industry would not be grossly impaired if the violent material were removed. The millions it now makes from such hire would still be made hiring other titles. The clientele would simply adjust their preference to what is being offered, which is just what is happening now. But who is to order or police tighter controls? And would they work? Such questions are not unanswerable, but get lost in arguments about civil rights and freedoms.

The Committee of Inquiry into Pornography in 1989 seems to share our view (149). It advocates the total banning of four categories of material: material that advocates or condones the sexual exploitation of children or young persons by adults; material which exploits children in its production; material that depicts acts of extreme violence or cruelty; and material that advocates or condones acts of extreme violence or cruelty. In addition, sexually violent material, and material depicting acts of 'bestiality, necrophilia, coprophilia or urolagia' (that is, sexual perversions relating to animals, cadavers, excretia, or urine) would also be banned unless there were mitigating factors such as artistic merit!

Would such a severe restriction not lead to blatant flouting of the law, an underground or black market in video porn? Well, we have that now. If anyone is 'into' one of these perversions (or any other), a few discreet enquiries will get them the goods they prefer. But when tastes become jaded, more salacious fare is sought. The Swedish government tried an open policy. After an active period, the trade in pornography seemed to die down. But that does not mean that there has been a reduction in viewing. The private world of Swedes remains private. The dilemma is real.

The day is almost upon us when, thanks to the satellite, the worst that the international porn industry can offer will pour out of the electronic orifices of our television sets. All we can do is to inform people, especially children, of what this stuff can do to them. We need to start at a very early age to teach youngsters discrimination so that they can make responsible choices. The Singers have devised and tested such curricula (227). We should also make our opinions clear to the media industries, the advertising industry; and especially to government. The consequences of the sex-and-violence trade damage us all.

But remember – who decided to let this stuff into our living-rooms? We all did.

# 14

## Alcohol

Throughout human history, alcohol has been associated with festivities and times of emotional release. Its deeper and more mystical use has been in religious sacraments. The consumption of alcohol has been common across cultures and over time but it has, till now, been a relatively scarce commodity. While many might have indulged at times of harvest, solstice or saturnalia, the regular use of quality alcohol was mostly confined to the wealthy or to the religious elite while the peasants drank beer, cider or sack. In Roman times, wine was associated with Bacchus, known by the Greeks as Dionysus, and with Saturn, the god of agriculture. The festivities were times of licentiousness; the last big party before winter was not the only occasion but it was the high point.

In the ancient world alcohol touched off release of exuberance, joy, and the relaxation of sexual inhibitions. Classically there was no particular association with violence.

It is the cultural assumption that alcohol disinhibits, provides for unbridled emotional release, and transforms the individual from his or her usual self, which has influenced the pattern of modern alcohol use in Western societies. Alcohol is 'timeout'. Alcohol declares a moral holiday. The drunken person is possessed by its spirits, which is why we use that term for alcohol in concentrated forms.

The uses of alcohol are legion, and there are numerous personal variations on the cultural norms. We wish to confine ourselves here to the use of alcohol as a permission for violence, the use of alcohol by those with violent propensities, and the persistence of a strong association between violence and the use or abuse of alcohol (115).

The prevailing tendency in alcohol policy has been to reverse the anachronistic legacy of the prohibition movement in the hope that liberalising the drinking hours, increasing the number of liquor outlets, and regionalising licensing will bring alcohol use under social rather than legal control, and increase responsible drinking behaviour.

The Department of Health has promulgated a health Charter with associated goals. These require regional health authorities to give high priority to reducing the menace of drunken drivers. While most are young men, drunk to the point of incompetence, and having accidents as a result, angry, aggressive or violent driving is frequently involved (12).

The pattern of alcohol use in New Zealand has its historical roots in frontier boozing and in exclusively male consumption in bars and in clubs. The prohibition movement of the 1880s, dominated by Kate Sheppard and the Women's Christian Temperance Union, played a major part in winning women the vote in 1893 but not in achieving prohibition (88, 254). Thereafter, New Zealanders voted, district by district, on whether their locality would be 'wet' or 'dry'. Most went wet but, in many areas that were dry, private clubs were established around male activities – miners' and working men's clubs, sports clubs and lodges. This aspect of New Zealand drinking gradually extended across the country. One result is that less than 20 per cent of alcohol is consumed in public bars, taverns or hotels; most alcohol in New Zealand is consumed in such clubs, homes or other private settings (34).

It is impossible to make generalisations about the kind of behaviour which people display when drunk. There are, of course, biochemical and physiological effects which are the same for everybody. These include the stimulating effects as the body converts the alcohol into energy. The result is a higher blood-sugar level, increased body heat, sweating, increased heart rate, vaso-dilation, and other physiological reactions which dissipate the additional energy. That energy surge may, itself, produce a feeling of well-being and increased response rate for a time. The secondary effects of continued consumption, loss of balance and of co-ordination of eyes and speech, vomiting and so on, are mostly the consequences of the direct action of alcohol on neural centres, whose functioning becomes increasingly depressed under the accumulation of toxins. The individual becomes drowsy, reaction time slows, and a general dysphoria replaces the previously elevated energy levels. That's all there is at the bio-chemical level. Long term physical damage to liver, brain, and neural function, with memory loss and dementia, are universal consequences of biochemical alcohol overload. All other effects are culturally patterned and induced.

In an important study of cultural variation, McAndrew and

Egerton report that in some societies drinking is associated with increasingly quiet behaviour, maximising the 'down phase' and the stuporous effects of the physiological process (130). In some societies, noisy, rowdy festive behaviour is very common, often associated with stimulation to sexual behaviour, but not necessarily with violence. In other societies again, violence emerges early and frequently in drunken behaviour. In almost all societies, the domestic, social use of alcohol is distinguished from occasions of heavier alcohol use, which are almost always characterised as times of license when whatever alcohol is expected to do, will dominate the behaviour. Thus, people who normally do not sing become opera stars for the night, the silent become garrulous, the modest obscene, and the meek do battle with the brave. Almost everywhere, the festive use of alcohol is regarded as time for a moral holiday when social *mores* may be suspended to a greater or lesser degree.

McAndrew and Egerton point out that drunken behaviour remains culturally patterned even when the drunken person 'goes out of control'. Thus, the expectations which govern drunken behaviour are learned, indeed over-learned, to the point where they are ascribed to nature. The fact that they are not natural but cultural must then be denied or suppressed, otherwise responsibility would rest with society and the individual. This is why it is so common, almost everywhere alcohol is used, for it to be made an excuse for the ensuing behaviour: 'He couldn't help it, he fell asleep'; 'She was so drunk, she couldn't remember'; 'Had he not been drunk, he would not have committed the rape', or murder, or whatever else.

Not every culture in the world had alcohol, or used alcohol. Many had no vessels in which to brew. A good number had other ways of producing altered states of consciousness. Many valued experiences associated with intoxication, however induced, and therefore also the substances associated with them, and patterned use and experience in highly ritualised and socialised ways.

Western patterns of alcohol use brought to the non-Western world the personal use of alcohol, associated with individual stress and strain, and the Western notion that one may drink to get away from something. After contact, alcohol use amongst the American Indians, Polynesians, Maori, and many other groups followed these Western patterns. Alcohol was added to other forces which led to the destruction of cultural controls. Western patterns included strong association between the elevated energy levels from alcohol use and fighting. This is a pattern particularly associated with the military, colonial frontiersmen, and other male associations. It is a gender-linked pattern. Folklore says that when drunk, both women and men may become sexual but some men become savage as well. Both reveal in booze their assumed 'real' nature.

Research supports the theory that drunken behaviour is learned (139). In one study, subjects did not know whether they were receiving their tonic water with or without vodka. Half were told that they were receiving alcohol, even though half of them were drinking plain tonic. All of this group acted as if they were drunk and were significantly more aggressive than the other group, who were told that they were drinking plain tonic. Half of these were, without their knowledge, given vodka as well. The levels of aggression among those who thought they were receiving no alcohol did not differ, even though half of them had in fact been drinking alcohol. Such are the tricks researchers play. But such too are the cultural tricks we all play with alcohol.

There are other similar studies (226, 243). There is also research that shows intoxicated people care less if their actions harm another (244).

Alcohol use is a sanction for the release of aggressive behaviour by those individuals in our society predisposed to violence. For this group, the association of alcohol and violence is habitual, repetitive, and predictable. We make matters worse by channelling drinking into situations where those with a personal pattern of violence can display it. The most conspicuous is the public tavern or bar, but the most dangerous is the home.

In the privacy of the home, private passions are expressed, no help is available, and others are reluctant to interfere. No area of the human environment is so copiously littered with available weapons. Yet public policy has almost forced alcohol consumption into domestic settings.

While not unique to New Zealand, the large barn-like premises designed for the maximum consumption of alcohol in the shortest possible time reached, in this country, staggering proportions. Their numbers are dwindling now but the legacy of the public bar remains. With the exception of Australia, no other country in the world institutionalised drinking in such unpleasant circumstances and in so irrational a manner. Furthermore, violence, the threat of violence, and fear of violence pervades the atmosphere of many of these places, in spite of the carpet on the floor and the rock band in the corner. While policy and management have emphasised smaller and more varied premises, the police continue to patrol the public bars where violence is still common.

Research on violence and drinking behaviour in New Zealand is sparse. One study by Ted and Nancy Graves in 1979 concluded that the strongest predictor of whether verbal confrontation would escalate into physical violence was the size of the drinking group of the person who started the fight (86). Bradbury researched all violent offences in one New Zealand city over a period of twenty months (29). Over half the assaults took place in licensed premises and many more offenders had been drinking prior to the offence. Bradbury indicates that violence is so accepted as appropriate behaviour in some drinking locations that this is what people go there for. The Graves' study emphasises that group loyalties are an important part of the social environment of public drinking places, where kinship and inter-group bonds catch people up in violent confrontations.

There is also research on misinterpretation of interpersonal cues in bar-room settings (244). The intoxicated person appears unable to process information very well, and in the rowdy, crowded conditions of a bar may misinterpret cues as aggressive or sexual, especially if there are threatening conditions or signs such as the wearing of gang insignia or arrogant behaviour.

New Zealand is less beer-sodden than it once was. The overall quantity of alcohol consumed has been dropping. The Business Indicators section of the Department of Statistics estimates alcohol consumption per head of population as follows:

1984    8.244 litres
1985    8.139 litres
1986    8.215 litres
1987    8.296 litres
1988    7.683 litres
1989    7.819 litres

The trend is consistent over age and socio-economic groupings. Alcohol consumption dropped by 10 per cent in 1988 – spirits and fortified wines were down by 20 per cent and beer by 10 per cent (*New Zealand Herald*, 3 January 1989).

Meanwhile, the level of violent offending has been increasing. This illustrates the point we have been making: that there is no necessary or inherent connection between alcohol and violence. The increased availability of liquor through a variety of outlets does not mean either that more alcohol will be consumed or that there will be an increase in alcohol-related violence. By some historical anachronism, Hamilton has had wine on sale in supermarkets for many years, as is frequently the case overseas. There is no evidence to suggest that alcohol-related violence in Hamilton is more frequent than anywhere else.

Problems will continue to exist where uncontrolled alcohol consumption occurs in places of large assembly, such as rock concerts, sporting events, and street gatherings such as New Year festivities.

Alcohol bans have been successfully introduced when public streets are used for New Year festivities and at most controllable events such as cricket matches. Individuals are not permitted to take alcohol into the game with them, but can buy it in rationed quantities within the grounds.

The subsequent analysis of the Aotea Square riots referred to earlier has been used in police training and initiation, but we do not see much evidence that the police will be better prepared next time around. Indeed, every year, in at least one New Zealand locality, baton charges, bloody heads, and mass arrests mark the close of one year and the beginning of the next. New Year's Eve is the closest approximation we have to Walpurgisnacht, when the warlocks and the witches of our own violent tendencies are momentarily unleashed as the clock strikes midnight.

Cheers!

*Remedies*

# 15
## Social Policy

The three great games of New Zealand social policy have been Happy Families, Fair Shares for All, and Keep the Natives Quiet. The first leads directly to state paternalism and female domestication; the second developed the whole structure of the regulated welfare state with its benefits, its levelling of differences, and its dependency; and the third led to a quite irrational, totally unsubstantiated belief that by some kind of enlightened and superior management we had achieved the best race relations in the world.

All three of these games have outlived their day but are still sustained by our cultural myths. They constitute a sort of wish list, drenched with nostalgia for days that never were, and which certainly will never come again.

New Zealanders no longer live in neat little nuclear families with Daddy-Boss-God at the head, and they have not done so, in increasingly large numbers, for a very long time. Yet politicians continue to talk about the restoration of family life as though the family was not the breeding place and the arena of much of the violence in our society. Especially in matters of social welfare, the family has been idealised as being sacrosanct, and everything possible has been done to keep families intact, often long after any semblance of viability has departed. For example, child protection teams have great difficulty in achieving speedy removal of children who have been abused because of the protections that surround parental rights. Nothing equivalent to the power of arrest has been granted to social workers who must deal with child abuse cases. They are not even able to demand that a child be produced so that he or she may be examined. They cannot, on their own judgement, remove a child for immediate medical examination. Incest offenders are often allowed to return to the family home even though the victim may still be living there.

We will not be able to develop a rational policy on violence until we have discarded some of the cultural baggage that we carry around concerning the traditional family and the rights and duties of parents. There is no sense in entrusting all parents with tasks that a sizeable minority are unable to fulfil.

Fair Shares For All may have been a New Zealand value from the very beginning but it found its full flowering in the climate of the Depression years and subsequent state socialism. But New Zealand did not become the great social laboratory of the world and put in place a fabric based on Fabian socialist policy because of some great ideological wave which swept across the nation. We were just tired of the other lot. And the alternative, the socialist ideologues, were skilful populist politicians and bureaucrats. They deserved a fair go.

Indeed, some of the deepest political principles of the first Labour administration had to be kept under wraps or in abeyance. Fraser and Semple had been total pacifists and the RSA would not have approved had this been emphasised. The socialist inner core believed in total state ownership and control of the means of production and supply, yet they could not immediately tackle the control on primary produce which lay in the hands of the stock and station agencies, the farm supply and produce transport firms, the big farm mortgage and insurance companies, and it was years before British ownership of the Bank of New Zealand was replaced by the state. Fair Shares For All included giving the capitalists a fair go too.

Labour was the party of the people who wanted work. The Depression produced its plurality, which they retained long enough to transform New Zealand along socialist lines and, in particular, to elevate mere egalitarianism into an ennobled concept of social justice for all. Even now, nobody knows quite what that means.

The social welfare state proved too costly. Given the nature of the resource base in New Zealand and the inefficiencies that crept into, and became part of, state enterprises, the structure was not economically viable. Inevitably during the later Muldoon years, and increasingly in the fourth Labour administration, inequalities of wealth became more extreme and the notion of social justice became even more elusive. Fair Shares For All meant Give Everyone A Go, and that led to First Up, Best Dressed, Every Man for Himself and the Devil Take the Hindmost – in other words, the politics of market forces and the new right.

New Zealand's racial policy has always been assimilationist (102), and we believe remains so in effect, if not in official word.

In order to silence Maori political protests in the 1920's there was token recognition that some Maori claims were justified and land questions required attention. Successive governments went along with the palliative measures of the Ngata era. Maori land incorporations restored tribal or hapu control but were never funded adequately to become effective or to upset rural wealth and interests. The establishment of trust boards to administer monies in compensation for historical wrongs was morally right but reparation payments were so miserly that trust board operations became trivial. The state was not about to set up agencies to compete with it for welfare loyalty. The Maori Education Foundation was essentially established on unclaimed rent monies that belonged to the Maori people anyway. For a while, there was a special school division for Maori people, but in 1951 they were told 'we are one people now' and the time had come to drop special provisions. From 1867 they were given their own department of state, titled Native and then later Maori Affairs which, because it had to be the Department of Everything, became the Department of Nothing Much At All. The people made use of it, but they did not respect it. Many blamed it for facilitating land sales, which it did through most of its history. It induced a dependence that sapped Maori initiative but never fulfilled Maori ambitions. It was a conduit for dependence funding in such areas as housing, marae subsidies, and preschooling, and a forum for status politics. But when the government proposed to take it away in 1987, a consortium of Maori opinion cried out for its retention (50, 51).

The department never had an effective or even clear social policy. It was not permitted to tackle the sources of violence amongst its clients, for these were the prime responsibilities of justice, the police, social welfare, and other agencies of state. As Maori resisted or refused to accept assimilationist pressure they were branded as failures, rejected by that which they were rejecting. Offered negative identity, the personal effect was to turn from or against the oppressive dominant culture. The seeds of violence are sown by such violation of the right to self-determination.

When the pacification of the Maori threatened to break down, the fourth Labour government (at least at first) seemed willing to adopt policies in Maori affairs such as the Waitangi Tribunal which were more than the equivalent of placating the natives with trinkets, blankets, and booze. But it quickly backed away from a Maori-driven programme for devolution to tribal authorities because the funding and jobs of existing branches of the State Services could not tolerate the proposed pace and direction of change. The Mahuta Committee on Devolution was sent packing in 1987 and replaced by a Pakeha official committee (107).

Jane Kelsey has analysed the Maori search for social justice over the life of the fourth Labour government (107). This has included the use of tribunals, courts and direct negotiations. There has been, as yet, little real improvement in the basic economic lot of Maori or in the social conditions which afflict the people. Government has spent more time dampening legitimate demands than meeting them.

Happy Families, Fair Shares for All, Keep the Natives Quiet – these three traditional planks in the platform of social policy have prevented the formulation of a trenchant and effective policy on violence in this  country. Hence, repeated select committee reports, special committee reports, committees of inquiry, and even the Royal Commission on Social Policy have not been able to formulate social policy that can become operational and programmatic.

A social policy is appropriate and effective when it establishes attainable goals which can be objectively assessed and evaluated. Anything else is merely mumbling and mouthing into the winds of social change in order to soothe an electorate which finds its own violence disturbing. Ordinary people will do everything they can to distance themselves from the responsibility for violence within them and around them. Politicians should not encourage or assist such deceptions. And yet, if they do not, they may well not be politicians for long. This is the basic dilemma of a rational social policy on violence. We scapegoat, we blame, we punish, we tinker, and we play games of emotional outrage. But we do not address the basic issues.

The business of public inquiry and committee reports on this matters is unending, so a brief summary must suffice.

During the last ten years there has been a parliamentary Select Committee into Violent Offending in 1979 (221), the Comber Report in 1981 on Gangs (165), the Penal Policy Review Committee in 1981 (172), the 1987 Committee of Inquiry into Violence (150), the Report of the Royal Commission on Social Policy in 1988 (210), and the Ministerial Committee of Inquiry into Prison Systems in 1989 (151).

The 1979 Select Committee into Violent Offending re-commended new family law legislation, expansion of the family support services of the Department of Social Welfare, and some changes to the liquor laws to strengthen rehabilitative treatment for alcohol abusers. The committee emphasised the link between liquor and violence but did nothing in practical terms about general education and re-education concerning violence (221).

The Comber Report on Gangs in 1981 sparked a variety of responses within a number of departments, including the provision of training and economic opportunities for co-operatives or community groups and street and community workers, and revealed ways in which project funding could come from a variety of sources. It is also led to changes in police operations, with an emphasis on preventive schemes such as Neighbourhood Watch (165). Some of these measures did help to prevent sporadic outbreaks of intense violence by gangs but did little to reduce moralistic media attention (108). Almost from the outset, the special work projects and other economic programmes for gang members were subjected to public and media suspicion and distrust and were finally rather dramatically terminated in 1988 after revelations by the police of the misuse of public funds.

Meanwhile, in areas such as Ruatoria and Wairoa, the nature of rural violence, Maori against Maori, began to appear as an extension of the urban experience of violent young men, who return, cultureless, to their rural roots, there to experience a renewed, doubled sense of alienation and frustration.

Gangs have become much more entrenched within prisons where much of their recruiting is done; they have adopted all the apurtenances of a sort of welfare society, lodge or residential club. They are not understood by, and therefore cannot be articulated with, the rest of society, which sees them chiefly in criminal mode.

Public agitation concerning the perceived increase in violence emanated from a Christchurch newspaper coupon campaign and led to the establishment of the Ministerial Committee of Inquiry into Violence in 1986. The committee's report ('the Roper report') and the extensive submissions by the Department of Justice present a comprehensive review of violent crime in New Zealand, but they also reveal an appalling dearth of information in some areas. For example, 'very little information is available on the incidence of domestic violence in New Zealand' (49 p. 6).

In some areas we disagree with the submissions made by the department (49). For example, they did not regard as conclusive the evidence of aggressive modelling in the media or the link between pornography and violence against women. The department gently slides away from the circumstances that led to the inquiry by saying that the advocacy of 'get tough' policies by those who are 'fed up' with crime and have become disillusioned by 'softness towards criminals' does not necessarily represent a majority opinion, nor always address the issues from an informed background. We agree – but the submission does not say what to do about people with such attitudes. It indicates that public opinion is not a guide to public policy on these matter – most people do not have any experience of violent offending, still less of prison and the punishment of criminals, and it hints that most could not care less.

The Department of Justice submissions make explicit re-commendations concerning the amelioration of the social conditions associated with violent offending, namely, economic disadvantage, inadequate housing, lack of political power, poor health, and stress. Other long-term goals, involving the media, more responsible use of alcohol, improving the position of women, and the removal of institutional racism, state a somewhat vague agenda. The recommendations rule out birching and capital punishment, disapprove of mandatory sentencing, and emphasise specialist treatment services, community-based sentencing, and reparational punishment (49).

These proposals are earnestly and seriously made, but they seem unlikely either to allay public fears or to address adequately the need to develop a social policy on violence. We note that the department's submissions do not abjure parental use of corporal punishment; nor, indeed, does the Roper report (49, 150).

The Mental Health Association also made a substantial submission to the committee of inquiry. It pointed out, and we would agree, that the causes of violence have been more than adequately researched and stresses the importance of developing a prevention programme with objectives that can be reasonably achieved. One such target which it identified is attitudes favourable to violence, such as the legitimation of coercive male authority, and the notion of the sanctity of the home as a male-dominated preserve. Three areas of prevention were identified: attitudes that support violence, frustrations which lead to it, and aspects of the reduction of control which causes violent events (145).

The Mental Health Foundation submission emphasised that national policy must be expressed in appropriate cultural terms for different groups and sectors in New Zealand society. There are, as we have already discussed, cultural legitimisations of violent behaviour that can only be addressed by change agents within these cultures. The anti-violence components of social policy need to be delivered within existing social programmes such as kohanga reo, alcohol detoxification programmes, and women's refuges. The Mental Health Foundation put strong emphasis on the issue of child abuse and the social permissions given to parents in the area of child punishment.

In our own submission we emphasised the causal factors of bad family experience and situational stresses, the importance of crisis intervention trouble-shooters, the need for better parenting by the state (as well as by parents), whose wards criminal offenders have so often been, the importance of removing children from bad homes and protecting them from abuse of all kinds. We called for a re-targetting of resources, the re-education of males, and a broad public information programme on how to handle aggression and thus reduce violence. We suggested that violent sports should receive no government subsidies, recognition or encouragement, that the media should cure itself of its addiction to violence, that prisons should be progressively replaced by community re-education centres, and that the police should have a special division trained in crisis intervention and counselling (201).

The Committee of Inquiry into Violence received many more submissions than those which we have discussed (150). In its final report the emphasis is clearly on what the politicians wanted, that is, recommendations on police and justice systems and practices, rather than a coherent body of social principles from which social policy could explicitly be stated and practices derived. We shall attempt this task, ourselves, in the last chapter.

Apart from these, the reports recommendations contain only peripheral suggestions, such as recommending that research be done on diet and food additives. We doubt that research of sufficient sensitivity could be done, and wonder if the diet of violent offenders differs greatly from that of most other New Zealanders. If junk-food is the enemy, roll on the vegetarian revolution, close the take-always and abandon the prisons! The report also implies that if only videos were adequately labelled, the problem of violent videos would somehow disappear since people would not inadvertently take home a violent video when they wanted a comedy or a drama! Other recommendations are worthy, but have less direct short-term relationship to violence. For example, the suggestion that funding for early childhood education should be increased, is worthy enough and can, in the long term, reduce criminal offending (94) but this is a long term matter when there is so urgent a need for funding of women's refuges, embryonic community and whanau therapy correction and rehabilitative systems, men's anger management groups and similar direct ways of dealing with the violent people around and amongst us.

In 1988 the much-heralded Royal Commission on Social Policy reported on its mission to reaffirm values and redefine policy goals for New Zealand well into the next century (210). Its brief was to assess how New Zealand lived up to its ideals of a fair society, and how government might achieve greater social well-being for all citizens. The brief contained statements of what government regards as the standards of a fair society: dignity and self-determination, sufficient living standards, genuine opportunity for all, fair distribution of wealth, and respect for cultural diversity. It also stated the social and economic foundations of New Zealand as a nation: democracy, freedom, equal rights, the role of law, collective responsibility, observance of the Treaty of Waitangi, a mixed economy, more responsibility, commitment to children, and gender equality.

The Royal Commission opened its doors to a veritable pilgrimage of petitioners bearing submissions. It undertook a survey of attitudes and values, and produced in five volumes a report of such length and complexity that we have not yet met anyone who has read it from cover to cover.

In all, the topic of violence receives but passing comment. There is a brief section on male behaviour in the abbreviated report, *Towards a Fair and Just Society* (209), but even this is inaccurate. It is simply not true to say that the true nature of male violence against women has only recently begun to be publicly acknowledged and investigated.

Suicides while in custody, overcrowding, and growing fear that the criminal justice system might be in danger of collapse led to the appointment of a Ministerial Committee of Inquiry into the Prison System under Sir Clinton Roper in 1988. On the one hand, the minister of justice believed that the vast bulk of prisoners were there because they should be, given the parameters of sentencing under which the system operates. On the other hand, government clearly wished to cut the costs of an escalating justice vote. Doubtless it also wanted to see a far wider range of community sentencing alternatives, and to employ a greater range of community rehabilitation and reformative agencies and experiences. Research for the committee found that 42 per cent of those in prison have been convicted of crimes of violence, and that many of those have six or more convictions. Twenty-five per cent of all prisoners were gang members but not all of these had committed violent offences. The report regards the starting point for rehabilitation and reparation to be the reconstruction of the lives of these offenders, not mere relocation to safe areas or holding pens till reoffending occurs (151).

The report of the Committee of Inquiry has made suggestions which, if implemented, would radically change the face of penal policy. The major emphasis is on rehabilitation, carried out in small, locally based 'habilitation centres'. The report is a mine of good sense and practicality. It wastes little time on criticising the lamentable business of imprisonment and moves directly to consider a wide range of alternatives to prison, changes in the climate and practice of imprisonment, management issues, staff training and specialist services. A great many of the 205 recommendations (with perhaps 100 sub-items) will require little additional cost but the comprehensive changes Roper considers desirable would constitute a revolution in penal practice and put New Zealand amongst the leading nations in such matters (151).

Government reaction has been minimal. Costs, it claimed, would be too great. But there are two factors of probably greater importance, public opinion and vested interest. The public are not likely to show much approval of proposals to close down prisons and relocate prisoners in community settings. The prison establishment, the capital base in facilities, the existing staff and management practices will need considerable time to be readjusted to the Roper way. Roper failed to show how costs might be reduced. Government lost interest.

This summary of a decade of official reports makes it clear that reporting on violence is not only different from, but appears to be preferred to, doing something about it. There is an absence of coherence, of any real sorting of practical solutions into longer-, medium- and short-term recommendations to specific programmes that can be implemented and evaluated. The reduction of social violence can, like any other area of public policy, be approached within a management-by-objectives strategy. At present, by any standard of efficiency, we are not coping with the phenomenon of violence.

This is certainly not because there is any lack of clear advice about what to do. Taken over all, since 1987 the Department of Justice has published some twenty-five studies, reports and background papers. All include recommendations. Massed together, just those in the two Roper reports, the Jackson report and the report on pornography present a powerful agenda for practical change which government might begin to address. But over-whelmingly the inescapable if cynical conclusion is that the most active thing we do about violence is to get someone to report on it while we all look other way.

# 16

# O Ratou Taonga Katoa

As we have said before, violence is endemic in all institutions in our society to a greater or lesser degree, and the violence of institutionalised racism is no exception. For example, many Maori complain that the present operations of the departments of social welfare, labour, health, and education simply fail to take account of their cultural needs. The response from the bureaucracy has been to ask what, if that is the case, they must now do.

The Maori response at the Hui Taumata summit conference in 1985 was 'give us some of the resources which you have and we will attend to these matters ourselves'. Although this seems a bold claim, it can be addressed. The proposals in the Department of Social Welfare's 1986 bi-cultural policy document Puao-te-Atatu (148); the opportunities which the implementation of the 1988 Taskforce to Review Education Administration (the Picot Report) will provide for Maori community control of education (241); Health Department recommendations for Maori participation in regional health policies; the Jackson report on the Maori and the criminal justice system (103) and the 1989 Roper report on prison systems (151), all add up to quite a radical change in overall social policy. Tardily and reluctantly, the government seems willing to address the issue of devolution of the previous Department of Maori Affairs, but there are still fears that to do so rapidly will disrupt present service delivery systems and pass them over to Maori authorities of unknown capacity.

Meanwhile, the debate over treaty issues will increasingly provide some public understanding even if, along the way, there is a backlash to deal with (38, 106, 107, 160, 258). The conscience of the country was reawakened in 1975 when the third Labour government enacted the Waitangi Tribunal Act (245). This law was motivated by genuine humanitarian desires to right the wrongs of the past and to make reparation for them. By legislative oversight, the 1975 act could apply only to violations of the treaty which occurred after the act was passed. The major Maori grievances, however, lay in the past. This omission was rectified by the fourth Labour government and the scope of the tribunal greatly expanded. The treaty debate and the tribunal proceedings have alerted everyone to past Maori grievances, but to date have made little difference to the lives of ordinary Maori people.

The facts of history are clear. The Maori people owned the resources, which the treaty guaranteed to them. The treaty, for all its several versions, had an elegant simplicity (168, 169). Leaving aside the preamble, it contains only three provisions. Article I gives sovereignty, Kawanatanga, the right to govern, to make laws, to the British Crown and its heirs and descendants. Everything that is derived from the state is an Article I function. Even the courts, which draw their authority from the Crown, are agents of that sovereignty. The treaty does not say in detail what sovereignty comprises, or what the Article I partner must do, but having established the notion of sovereignty the Crown goes on to make guarantees to the rangatira, representing the Maori people, in Articles II and III.

Article II recognises the rights of rangatiratanga, the authority of the chiefs, in their ownership of, and right to manage, their own resources and everything they valued, both material and non-material – o ratou taonga katoa.

Article III simply states that the Crown will guarantee to Maori people all the rights and privileges of citizenship. (38).

The treaty has never been ratified in statute nor has it been explicitly revoked. It has merely been neglected, ignored, and dishonoured. Nevertheless, it remains the primary contract by right of which non-Maori people are here in New Zealand. The treaty was blatantly violated both before and after the land wars, until it was judicially declared a nullity by Judge Pendergrast in 1877, (168). The so-called protective institutions, the Department of Maori Affairs and the Maori Land Court, became agencies to facilitate further dispossession. After World War II, government policy was to relocate Maori people in urban areas where there was work for the growing population. The migration policy was essentially economically based, and not motivated by greed, as had been the land wars and other acquisitions. The government of the 1950s and thereafter considered that Maori employment, housing, and other social needs could be better met in urban areas. Yet further land loss ensued.

We now see this policy to have been wrong. It eroded the tribal

and rural basis of Maori society which depended upon collectivity
and replaced it with an imposed individualism. The consequence is
that many young Maori have grown up in an alien cultural environment in a society in which they have no stake. The
government's advisors saw little hope of full employment (in their
terms) for rural Maori and set up policies to move them to where
they could have jobs and houses. The inducement to move was a
modern house on a cheap loan from the Department of Maori
Affairs, and an assured job, also provided by the department. The
'choice' was no choice at all. Nor was the full employment promise
fulfilled.

Repeatedly, Maori people sought redress for their ancient wrongs,
and got nowhere. The Sim Commission of 1928 declared the
confiscation of Maori land in Taranaki and the Waikato (almost
three million acres in all) to have been excessive and immoral, but
Maori had to wait until the late 1980s before it was acknowledged to
be illegal.

Think now of this. Imagine that you live in a country which you,
your whanau, and your ancestors owned, cared for, loved, and
protected. Then by force and chicanery, substantial sections of this
land were taken, more still acquired through dubious forced sales
until you are alien within your own territory. Imagine still further
that church and state combined to undermine the system of social
control which had protected your society from aberrant individuals
and interpersonal violence, and thus totally disrupted the balance
between the individual and collective social controls. Imagine that
you were asked, for fifty years, to believe that the state would
benevolently replace these things, only to find that the state did not,
did not even know how, that the state cared more for its own kind
than for your people, and that slowly your life was sliding towards
hopelessness and despair. How, then, would you feel?

Such conditions might provoke their victims to lash out against
the symbols, structures and persons of the authority which allowed
them to arise. A history of violence leaves a legacy of resentment. In
such conditions, arson and the molotov cocktail can become
personal tools of revenge. Where no tribal authority has power to
intervene in such personal urges, group hostilities or long-standing
family feuds may erupt in violence. In their own history these were a
warrior people in whose tradition it was honourable to fight and
then to fight again. In the past, the violence was contained by
systems of control, of rahui, tapu, utu and muru, by collective
decisions or by the authority of chiefs (151). Now it breaks out, like
fire in the root of the fern.

Maori leaders stated at the Hui Taumata that the current
situation can be remedied by a rapid programme of reconstruction

of Maori authority patterns, starting from a tribal base. That has been the basis of repeated tribal statements and submissions on legislation affecting Maori affairs. There is an opposing view, much favoured by conservative political spokespeople, who believe that alienated urban Maori populations cannot respond to tribal control which they believe is essentially rural in nature and origin (242). We know of no evidence that this view is correct. The multiplicity of tribal groups in urban areas can be dealt with by building tribal associations and allegiances, rather than by continuing with policies which amorphously attempt to integrate Maori into some kind of pan-tribal identity. There never was such an identity, and most of the ordinary mechanisms of Maori culture cannot be made to work on such a basis. Such policies are not unlike the assimilationist pressures of the 1950s and 1960s (for example, the Hunn report) which envisaged all Maori ultimately becoming individuals within an integrated New Zealand society. That was a policy that was tried and which failed.

What, then, should be done? Violence by Maori offenders can only be reduced if the position of the Maori people is improved (103, 151). There are three immediate avenues that must be pursued. They are economic opportunity, education, and power sharing.

Economic opportunity must restore to the Maori people control of their own resources so that they are not merely subservient to a monocultural commercial and authority structure. Poverty will always engender helplessness and resentment. Unemployment adds to poverty, and provides extra time and energy with nothing to do. Until Maori people have adequate resources, any talk of cultural renaissance or reconstruction is just empty words.

Maori people have their own ideas of how the unemployed might be occupied. What they have not been able to do is persuade the institutions of government to put such programmes into operation. Maori land requires massive labour for conservation, rehabilitation, and development, and someone must pay for that. Marae facilities throughout the country need repair and extension; historic buildings need careful restoration. The concept of the marae as a set of community facilities that will service all kinds of needs from before birth until after death is capable of great creative expansion. Facilities such as houses for the old, health centres, young people's houses, training centres, tourist and entertainment complexes, educational facilities, recreation and sporting centres, small business ventures could all be part of a modern marae. All the major cities in New Zealand have far too few marae complexes. Auckland alone probably needs a further fifteen to twenty at the present time. Building these facilities as well as running them would utilise a considerable labour force, and to those who say that the cost would be prohibitive, the answer that many Maori people give is that the present costs of sustaining Maori people on welfare benefits, plus the costs of institutional care which has no positive outcome, are also enormous; the Maori Economic Development Commission estimated somewhere in the vicinity of $600 million a year (55). This negative spending needs to be progressively reduced and money made available for positive programmes under Maori control.

To undertake this restructuring two kinds of education will be needed. The next generation of Maori people passing through the education system needs to see that there will be career alternatives working in, and for, their tribal organisations. Tribal authorities can right now state the targets for the next five years if Maori people are to assume control of economic resources, engage in social and environmental planning, and impact on the structure of New Zealand society as its institutions change in response to the demand for tribal system recognition, or tino rangatiratanga.

The second kind of education would create a climate of understanding in which such change could occur. This begins with a thorough understanding of the treaty and a rewriting of our history.

Power sharing must be accomplished not only through devolution but also by allowing Maori philosophy, values, and viewpoints to penetrate mainstream institutions, by real reassessment of the constitutional challenge (160). Alongside every bureaucrat there needs to be a monitor who constantly reminds: 'Correct your actions in treaty terms; check that you are not violating the cultural rights and integrity of anyone; is this decision consistent with the ideal of a bicultural society?'

If we seem to have departed somewhat from the theme of violence it is because head-on solutions are unlikely to be successful or peaceful. We do not anticipate that the streets of Auckland will soon resemble those of Northern Ireland, but there is this significant parallel: generations of the deprived will rear generations like themselves, and attitudes will harden on both sides. Those of any race who have no stake in the society around them may wreck it. Knowing what we know about violence and control in our society, we can predict that there will be increasing demand for repression and coercion against minority cultures unless we change things now, not just with good intent, but to good effect.

# 17

# Becoming Less Violent

For thirty years New Zealand has been becoming more obviously violent. Domestic violence has always been here, but is almost certainly increasing, along with child abuse and neglect and the other precursors of violent offending. We have cluttered up our entertainment media with violent images and brought international lawlessness and terror into our living-rooms. We persist in irrational methods of imprisonment and hopelessly outdated penal policies.

Riots in prisons and the torching of schools and other public places are clear signs that unless institutions change they will be attacked. They create violence; they are the public arenas for the enactment of such violence.

Such escalation is making our country more tense, less safe, and less pleasant. However, we may not yet have reached the point of critical consciousness where the desire to change is matched by the will to change and the means are found to make change possible.

Those who might be directing change are circumscribed in what they can do by past investment in existing institutions. We are unlikely to be able to close Paremoremo overnight. Politicians are also limited by what they think the electorate will tolerate, or because the social change required would be socially unacceptable – for instance, the banning of rugby.

But we are not politicians, simply New Zealanders who care greatly for our country and the New Zealand way of life. So we can write a programme for change in the hope that by doing so, we will help to bring about that critical state of consciousness. The changes that are easy to make should become the short-term targets. They lead on logically to wider programmes of reform and ultimately to the whole paradigm of change that is the long-term objective.

There are three phases in making change. First of all, there must be desire on the part of someone that a change be made. If the person wanting the change is not the person who has to make the change, nothing will happen until the latter has been motivated or persuaded. Secondly, there is the process of making the change itself, which requires a clear programme, graduated steps, and lots of support. Finally, the change must be fixed in behavioural or social terms and this may require legislation at the national level, new forms of social control, and, most of all, reinforcement, that is, rewards for behaving in the approved manner.

Figure 2 represents a proposal for change in terms of different levels: the personal, the interpersonal, the social, the cultural, and the general environmental. Naturally, the real world does not layer itself in this way, and as we talk about, for example, changes in the male role, we will be talking about all levels at once. But we must begin somewhere.

At the personal level, most people have learnt to deal with anger and frustration in some way or another. In most cases we have very little idea of how we learned our existing patterns. Unless we find ourselves in a crisis we hardly ever bother to evaluate whether what we are doing is efficient and whether there are better ways. While most of us are not violent most of the time, a recipe could be written  to tip everyone into outward or inward destructiveness. Years ago, Laurence Frank (67), carried away by enthusiasm for psychoanalysis, proposed that everyone should have the chance therapeutically to clear themselves of their past. Karen Horney in her useful little book, *Self Analysis* (98), said that everyone could benefit from a programme of reassessment or reprogramming. Therapy cults, religious cults, retreats, executive mutual evaluation sessions in business settings are all ventures along this track. But therapy for everyone is too wide and expensive a target to achieve. Anyway, we are not too sure that therapists always know what they are doing! But we must provide change conditions for those who realise that they need to change, or for whom change is a contingency, an alternative to loss of liberty or other social sanction.

We know the targets and the techniques; there is a lot of information available about training and retraining in anger management, communication skills, handling conflict and frustration, and developing greater sensitivity. Men Against Rape, Men Against Violence, and similar change and support groups and workshops are already operating, although not everywhere, and not all the time. Relief and release models for tension reduction, such as a massage, or a good exhausting work-out or run, are ways of dealing with a

## Figure 2

## A Programme for Change: Targets and Means

| Sector | Targets | Means |
|---|---|---|
| Personal | To remove present supports and permissions for violent acts<br>To create conditions for personal change through<br>  – learning about violence<br>  – anger management<br>  – communication skills<br>  – conflict and frustration<br>    management<br>  – sensitivity training | Men's groups<br>Workshops<br>Support groups<br>Crisis centres<br>Humanise working<br>  conditions |
| Interpersonal | To improve partnering<br>To improve and share parenting<br>To change attitudes<br><br>To eliminate racism<br>To eliminate sexism | Parent education<br>Family support centres<br>  in schools and neigh-<br>  bourhood<br>Core curriculum in<br>  interpersonal relations<br>Acknowledge violence<br>Remove coercive controls in<br>  schools<br>Teach conflict resolution |
| Societal | To remove social and economic basis of inequity<br>  poverty<br>  unemployment<br>  poor housing<br>To improve social servicing | Reallocate resources to social<br>  goals<br>Collectivise all kinds of care<br>Community accountability<br>  for state servicing<br>Strengthen and activate<br>  community servicing in<br>  part-time and voluntary<br>  work<br>Community rehabilitation<br>  programmes |
| Cultural | To recognise alternatives to<br>  the Legal system<br>  the Penal system<br>  the Policing system<br>To restructure the male role<br>To recognise alternatives in parenting | Develop a core code for all<br>  social institutions based<br>  on non-violence<br>    reduction in<br>    racism<br>    sexism<br>Implement programmes of<br>  change by objectives |
| The non-violent environment | To detoxify the environment<br>Alternative challenges<br>To promote non-violent sports<br>To withdraw support from any violent acts or aspects<br>To clean up the media<br>To promote sensible alcohol use | General vigilance<br>Legislative changes<br><br><br>Adopt a plan to detoxify the<br>  media. |

personal crisis that may be building up, although they do not remove causes or teach desirable ways of solving the crisis. Tackling personal vulnerability must be part of the short-term focus. The personal quality needed here is tender strength, not toughness, and young people need to have before them good models of strong people who have survived mental breakdown or other emotional crises. Who are the resilient, gentle, strong men in the New Zealand tradition? Can we not put their images in front of young people instead of portraits of rugby heroes?

Assertiveness training, which is a well developed technique in women's groups, needs to be more universally available. Women generally go to assertiveness training because they feel they are too submissive or dependent. Men are more likely to need to learn to appreciate the consequences of their aggressive behaviour and to learn ways of modifying it. Men's groups can help men to learn to express their anger appropriately.

At the interpersonal level, we need to teach people how to make partnerships in which mutual dependency is acknowledged, but where the partnership is not unbalanced. There are many men who are unable to sustain non-sexual relationships with women and who fear intimacy with other men for sexual reasons. As young people grow up they need opportunities to learn how to achieve closeness and companionship. The violent person is often a person with poor social skills and few or no friends – the 'man alone' model is a dangerous one.

The high school is the prime location for producing a better model for male-female relationships. Single-sex schools could organise workshops with other schools.

The past emphasis on traditional marital relationships is anachronistic. We may be approaching a post-marriage era when individuals will move through partnerships according to preference or need and without seeking legal or religious recognition of the relationship.

We need partnerships for each other's company but also for the future if we wish to become parents. The basic models of parenting in New Zealand, as projected by parents' centres, playcentres and Plunket, emphasise the nurturing qualities of the traditional female role. Their clientele has been largely white and middleclass. Even though they are all opposed to physical punishment they have not made a significant impact upon the prevalence of physical punishment in the pattern of 'proper' parenting; they have not been able to carry their  message into the sectors of society where the potential for violence is greatest. They tend also to be monocultural.

Parenting needs to be made continuous with all other experiences of learning to care. The kind of parent you become is patterned by all the experiences you have had of other people caring for you. Children, from the earliest age, need good parenting models around them – especially if their own are not so good at it.

Human societies through history have found many ways of affording children the experience of alternative parenting. We have dropped these opportunities out of our social systems, but we can still put them back. We can start by encouraging extended families to participate in settings such as childcare centres, preschools, primary schools, and high schools.

That many hands make light work is not a hollow aphorism. It is well established that the more parenting is shared, the more helping hands per child, the lesser the load and the greater the parental warmth (27). Many parents means many alternatives in times of stress, and the higher level of supervision means more effective learning of personal and social control.

At the interpersonal level, the broad target of attitude change can be accomplished through a variety of social institutions and means. The aims are, first of all, to be more open about violence, to acknowledge when it occurs and why, and to recognise that the responsibility for preventing it rests with each individual.

The second aim involves understanding how social control operates in a society like ours, and the need to replace coercive, oppressive, restrictive, and punitive controls with affirmative and positive experiences in which desirable behaviour is praised and rewarded. What we are calling for here is the establishment of a code which rejects force, and creates optimal conditions for discussion, persuasion, negotiation, and accommodation. While this may sound like a facile formulation we recognise that the scope of it is enormous and the change almost revolutionary. But we are not alone in this. Taken over-all this is the import of the hundreds of recommendations in the Roper Report on Prisons (151). In 1977 Napier City set up a pilot programme based on such a code (151 pp. 105–106).

Racism and sexism both generate violence at the personal, the interpersonal, and the institutional level. Programmes for the elimination of racism are already established in institutions such as the Race Relations Office, the Social Welfare Department's report *Puao-te-Atatu* (148), the affirmative action programme of the State Services Commission, and Project Waitangi (258). The agenda is clear and public. Some high schools run anti-racism workshops at the interpersonal level, but most people feel safer dealing with racism at the institutional level. Of course it should be dealt with there as well, but such programmes will not succeed unless personal attitude change occurs first.

Societies which are sexist are also the most violent, and violence is most common in areas which are either exclusively male, or where the power imbalance between the sexes is greatest (218). The elimination of sexism is a definable social goal; progress towards it can and should be monitored.

What means are there for eliminating interpersonal violence? We need to fashion comprehensive intermediate and high school programmes in interpersonal skills, and carry the practice of good interpersonal relations right through the school system. The classroom should be a laboratory for showing children what is going on between them and how to manage their human relationships. We teach children how to handle mathematical concepts, so why can we not teach them how to handle their emotions? Some people may claim that this is a parental responsibility in which the schools should have no part. But children learn in all situations, and from all those with whom they interact. Much of the time they are not with their parents, and many parents do not know how to handle their own emotions, especially the violent ones.

The school curriculum could cover everything we have discussed in this book, appropriately presented. Subjects such as the linkage between sex and violence, or pornography and rape, can be dealt with in the context of education for healthy sexual attitudes. Our children now live in a wide open world where television is providing them with as much, or more, information than either school or parents normally provide. Sexuality and violence are not hidden from them. It is therefore essential that we present healthy models and develop healthy attitudes through all the agencies at our disposal.

We need to work now towards societal change on the basis of the same models we already have for interpersonal change. Years ago we suggested that support centres should be located in every primary school. Support should be available for parents from pregnancy right through the school system. Many American high schools now provide for teenage mothers to continue their education during their pregnancy and beyond, rather than making them run away and hide and take correspondence lessons. If we really valued education for all, we would not deny pregnant teenagers access to it. And the experience of providing child care within a high school offers the opportunity for parenting education for everyone, but especially for the mothers themselves.

Social, economic, racial and gender inequalities are major sources of frustration and deprivation which lie behind much of the violence in our society. The dilemma of social policy has always been that of making general provisions which will truly service the needy without lumbering the system with free-loaders.

The genuine alleviation of social difficulties requires close and attentive servicing which bureaucratic institutions find hard to provide and still more so in times of economic hardship. The economy cannot support increased social services unless there is a redistribution of funding from non-social service areas such as defence; without such diversion of public money, the problem becomes one of how better to spend the welfare dollar and of redesigning delivery systems.

As we saw with Maori devolution, our current social institutions are heavily committed to negative funding and existing jobs and practices. If we were to take the $35,000 per year that it costs to keep a violent offender in prison and spend it on community-based rehabilitation, we might be able to move quickly from custodial to remedial care and from negative to positive spending.

We think both access to and quality of social services would be improved if a neighbourhood-based policy were adopted. Why not reopen disused post offices as social service centres? Why not relocate the health, welfare, geriatric, and parenting support services in the neighbourhood institutions of childcare centres, kohanga reo, community houses, and the work-place? Recruitment of part-time and voluntary staff to assist the professional agencies would then be facilitated, and there would be better access to domestic situations needing help with drug and alcohol detoxification, housing, and protection against domestic violence.

Although still in its infancy, the child protection team provides a multi-disciplinary model. We have to shift the focus from dealing with the problem to dealing with the people for whom it is a problem. Sometimes these are not the clients at all, but the so-called care-givers who may not know where to go for help. Relocating services back into the community can begin to reactivate and re-establish a culture of caring. Parentline is a good model.

Currently we struggle to give barely more than token recognition to the new institutional structures – rape crisis centres, women's refuges, men's groups, parent counselling groups. If we can give away education, at least in part, to the care of parental committees and charters, why can't we do the same for the institutions of welfare? The usual answer is, of course, that the community does not have the structures, the trained people, the facilities, and the resources to run welfare services as a school board of trustees might run a school. So long as we go on saying that, we fulfil our own prophecy.

But we should at least make beginnings, and require of existing service departments that they achieve community restructuring targets in methodical and progressive ways. Let labour, housing, and social welfare set their own goals, as has been suggested for Maori tribal authorities, and their own timetable. The overall objective should be to reduce the central and regional bureaucracy to a lean, efficient funding mechanism and get the resources into community hands as fact as possible.

We are confronting the problem of cultural inertia. Many New Zealanders are already asking why we have a military system of defence when trade and aid might achieve for us the same security – and they are as likely to be doing so on the basis of a hard-headed business analysis as on one of pacificism. The Roper report asked the same question about the prison system – why do we need it at all? A similar set of questions was raised by the Jackson report on racism and justice. And when Prime Minister Lange established the Royal Commission on Social Policy he hoped for clear principles, which could be applied to every institution and from which new practices might flow.

Those who run the institutions of our society should seek to remove from their practices anything which is itself violent and to take up the challenge of prevention. This means that all existing legislation must be scrutinised. There are already welcome changes in judicial practices such as those for child testimony in sexual abuse cases, and we have, at last, removed the death penalty from the statutes.

All the institutions of society must be held accountable in terms of the desired changes. We should be open about the causes and the prevalence of violence; we should seek collective, bi-cultural, and multi-cultural answers to the problems it creates; violent aspects of the male stereotype should be progressively reduced until they are finally eliminated. We must cease to dramatise, romanticise, glorify or sensationalise violence in its many forms, from self defence through sport to war.

As we have become more aware of the dangers of environmental degradation so something has arisen that one might regard as a set of environmental ethics. Slowly, we may recover biological balance as we obey these new and emerging rules of what thou shall and shalt not do. About some of these rules we must be firm, tough minded, indeed adamant. The same kind of change is needed to reduce violence.

Most of us are not law abiding because we know the law but because other things control our behaviour, those around us, moral standards within us, or we simply live where violent law breaking does not occur. We receive non-violent messages all the time as well as the violent ones. They come from those we love, those we respect, those we fear. They come most strongly, as we grow, when someone cares enough about us to explain and support us while we change. For all of the Christian era an ethic of non-violence has been preached but limited by its theological origin.

A secular non-violent ethic will produce its own challenges and will force modification of some currently held rights, such as the right to keep firearms in one's home or to engage in sports that cause physical injury to others. Some rights have already been relinquished, although there are men who still regard women as their exclusive possessions or who become angry over the matrimonial property law or at suggestions that sexual harassment is no longer acceptable.

For the young and energetic, offenders or not, we may need what William James called 'the moral equivalent of war' (104) – hard experience in tough environments, such as the project in which Graeme Dingle took a group of young offenders through the wilderness areas of both islands. The army incorporates such elements into its programmes for the unemployed, and a number of Maori trust boards wish to do the same. The recently formed Conservation Corps is a slight beginning but is unlikely to touch hard-core violent offenders. While we are clearing up the environment, why not clean up the media at the same time? James wrote his essay as a challenge to the peace movement, now, in its modern form, nearly 100 years old. After World War II, the War on Want paralleled the idea Lyndon Johnson in his Great Society policy spoke of as the war on poverty. Our own country has in its environmental issues, want and poverty, many challenges alternative to 'punch-ups', playing chicken,  cop-baiting and other kinds of acting-out.

All this is not a prescription for a society that is puritanical, bland and dull. A safe environment need not be an unexciting one. Our artists and adventurers may still employ their energies and their imaginations. The intensity of human emotions and experience will not be any the less.

We said at the outset that we would be seeking to find and to present the patterns that connect violent phenomena in New Zealand. There are several running as themes throughout this book. One is the cultural definition of male role behaviour and the image of the female reflected by it. Slowly this is changing. Another is the theme of retribution, punishment and justifications for vindictiveness. In schools, prisons, families this is changing, too. Our proneness to explain behaviour in terms of biological determination, to resort to explanations or attribution of cause, in animal urges or genetic or racial inheritance, is a third. Here change is slower. Even more entrenched and resistant are notions of the right to privacy, individual responsibility and personal freedoms. Cherished as these are as culture verities, they  contribute to our violent society.

Is there another order of pattern connecting these patterns? Bateson would have said that there is and that when we find it change will be easier and more rapid (18). One such is that we define change as difficult, disruptive and therefore slow. Simultaneous action on all aspects of the patterning of violence in our society is possible, practical and realisable. If we really seek change, change will occur.

When the yoke of violence falls away, what follows is a release of the spirit from past encumbrances and from an incubus that was not there of necessity at all. One way to stop a nightmare is to wake up.

# Epilogue

Most people regard violent behaviour as irrational. What does this mean? It certainly does not mean that we do not understand why it occurs. The whole of this and many other books show that this is not the case. Violent behaviour can be understood both as a personal and a social behaviour when we take trouble enough to apply human reason to the process of understanding.

For some it means that violent behaviour occurs beyond the ordinary limits of control, without thought, but we know that the perpetrators of domestic violence carefully locate their blows on parts of the woman's body where they will not show, and repeatedly enact intimidatory scenarios with a clear headed objective of physical and sexual domination.

Violence is not irrational. To believe otherwise places change beyond the capacity of human reason, planning and programming. Reason and reasonableness are our criteria for the process of planning for change.

In the last five years reason and good sense have prevailed in many areas of the management of violent behaviour. We will emphasise these positive trends, not because we wish to deny continuing phenomena that have such dreadful consequences, from child abuse to multiple murder, but because we believe that awareness about violence has been raised to the level where change is possible. We are certainly more conscious of the daily load of violence and its consequences which our society is carrying and so, many more people are asking, what can be done?

There have been many dramatic stimuli to arouse us from the

nightmare: the Aramoana massacre, the Delcelia Witika case, mass murders at Paerata and Masterton, public revelation of scandalous child sexual abuse. But as a society no one has yet presented us with a rational and systematic programme for the reduction of violence by coordinated, national action.

Instead, the focus continues to be primarily on violent crime, as if that was all that violence encompassed, on the law as a mechanism for the intervention and control, and on the more outrageous offences, such as sensational cases of rape or violence against children. The law has a wider role than this. Jurisprudence, the wisdom of law, looks beyond single situations, crimes or offenders to view social and political objectives beyond the merely judicial. The law can change attitudes, but often does not.

Following the 1987 Roper Report, governments have introduced changes to legislation dealing with parole, bail, mandatory minimum sentences, firearms, knives, other offensive weapons and disabling substances, all of which changes appear, so far, to have made virtually no difference to the crime rates (265). Criminologists point out that offenders do not expect to get caught and that increasing penalties is rarely effective (275). Feminists oppose the proposed increase in the penalty for rape from 14 to 20 years because only a change in misogynist and patriarchal attitudes will reduce the frequency of rape. They point out that an increase in penalty may increase the likelihood of murder of the victim.

The power of the law to change attitudes is the cornerstone of civil rights legislation. It has also effectively been demonstrated in the area of assault on children. Sweden has been followed by Norway, Denmark, Finland and Austria in banning the parental use of physical punishment. Physical abuse of children subsequently reduced (276).

New Zealand finally outlawed corporal punishment in school in 1990. Two years later, when a private member's bill sought to restore the right of decision to Boards of Trustees, the teaching profession turned from this proposal with disdain. Even prominent educators who, just a few years prior to the legal change, had been endorsing corporal punishment as a last resort, now firmly reject its reintroduction. Other factors than just legal changes were at work here, of course, but when the law appeals to a wider humanitarian ideal and offers a real protection, we see its power for permanent change.

The real battle, however, remains on the home front. The Crimes Act still gives parents permission to hit children with 'reasonable force'. The research unequivocally shows there is danger to children in this (276). Most child abuse is committed by ordinary parents, who, this time, went too far in the course of their ordinary discipline. Physically punishing children is dangerous. In the United Kingdom surveys of agencies dealing with child abuse (268) reached the conclusion that 'there are relatively few cases of deliberate cruelty and the majority of cases dealt with represent over-chastisement or loss of control in administering physical punishment' (p.10). The *normal* explanation of child abuse is physical punishment. The converse, that all physical punishment is child abuse, would clearly be rejected by most people as absurd yet those who use it 'mildly' can never be sure that they will never lose control and should, in any case, give it up so that there is moral and legal pressure on those who use it abusively.

The problem both in child abuse research, and in prosecution, is where should the line be drawn. Because this cannot be reasonably answered, the question is pointless. While most parents continue to hit most children, some will always be at risk. Clearly the law is protecting the rights of parents, not the rights of children. In order to protect children we give up many rights. We all must fence our swimming pools even though we may not have children. The time has come to stop hitting defenceless children.

The Commissioner for Children has now indicated a readiness to assume responsibility for advocacy on this important issue (270). The time has come for legal action on this matter. The first step would be to change Section 59 of the Crimes Act and at the same time mount an extensive education campaign to teach positive parenting.

In 1989 the Labour government established the office of the Commissioner for Children to promote child policy for New Zealand and to generally ensure progress towards the ratification of the United Nations Convention on the Rights of the Child. This was an important step forward, particularly since in 1988 a major enactment redefined public policy in respect of children and their families: the Children, Young Persons and their Families Act. This piece of legislation has survived an intensive review and is gaining attention and admiration world wide (273).

The Act provides more than simply child protection. It establishes procedures for dealing with matters of youth justice. It is a significant step away from the previous trend to increasing bureaucratisation and legal procedures. It balances these with negotiation, consultation with family and community and social agency involvement. The rights of the child are now to be seen in the context of those whose daily duty it is to uphold, foster and protect them, and not in isolation.

The office of the Commissioner for Children and the Act, together, are radically changing what happens when children, for example, go to court (either as a victim or offender), are caught up in a marital breakdown or otherwise become involved in violent situations.

However, there is still a long way to go before the public really begins to catch up with the progress which the Office and the Act

represent. But progress is being made. Police Youth Aid have wel-
comed the new situation and work comfortably within it. However,
front-line police and the Police Association have called for changes,
which, if passed, will erode the rights of young people by allowing
them to be questioned before arrest and without an explanation of
their rights.

The other area of change currently contemplated is the question
of mandatory reporting of suspected child abuse. This was strongly
recommended by the Mason Report but is opposed by some on
the grounds that compulsion is not necessary and that sufficient
progress has already been made towards adequate reporting. Some
believe that compulsion will have the reverse effect, inducing a fear
of entanglement in the legal process. The Association of Social
Workers fears that there will be inadequate training and resources to
deal with the flood of cases that would follow the introduction of
mandatory reporting. They are particularly concerned about sensitivity in the investigation process, particularly in sexual abuse cases.

The counterview has prevailed in many overseas countries: that
services will never be adequate to meet the need until the extent of
the need is known. Thè strong development of voluntary organisations which support and assist in cases of family distress, such as
Parentline, should be reassuring. The professionals are not on their
own, they are backed by many caring voluntary groups.

Mandatory reporting is a moral responsibility which should no
longer be denied or evaded. There are costs and they must be paid
because, above all, children must be protected.

By far the most promising development in the last five years has
been the rapid growth of direct action by men to reduce male violence. The cultural construction of the ideology of violence, the worship of heroes and warriors, has largely been a male enterprise. It is
sustained to entrench male egos, privileges and assumed rights. It
provides the latent permission for the commission of most of the violence which occurs in our society (150). Women and children and
others relatively weak and powerless in our society, all of whom are
potential victims, are rarely in a position to do anything about the
situation. This is why survivor support groups are so isolated,
powerless and poorly funded.

Men must become responsible for their own behaviour. What is
so promising is that this is now happening. For example, the sociolo-
gist Greg Newbold calls upon other men to reject sports such as
football, boxing, and the portrayal of violence and conflict between
men in television and film (270).

Men for Non-Violence now run courses and workshops to enable
men to deal with their anger and aggression (262). Such courses
are now being carried into school programmes. The object is to

focus on power and control, rather than just with anger management. The latter focuses only on behaviour change while the real problem is what happens when male dominance is threatened or challenged. No one seeks to be angry but the desire to have power over another, to dominate, to control, lies behind all the invasive and damaging strategies that men are trained, encouraged or permitted to employ. These programmes ask men to ask themselves how, why and when they are seeking power and control, and what the proper exercise of authority should be (283).

The same realisation lies behind the highly effective programme which is being trialled in Hamilton over a three year period (280, 281). The Hamilton Abuse Intervention Pilot Programme (HAIPP) is sponsored by the Family Violence Prevention Coordinating Committee which was set up to bring together the wide range of services which have a role in reducing domestic violence, including the police, government departments and community agencies such as women's refuges and Men for Non-Violence.

HAIPP approaches the problem of domestic violence by first coordinating with the police so that whenever there is a domestic assault there is an automatic arrest. Secondly, if convicted, the abusers must undertake a twenty-six week education programme which, if breached, results in immediate court sanction. Thirdly, the victims receive immediate support and safety, legal services and they are offered the chance to participate in a women's programme.

Results so far show an increase in arrest rates with the women reporting an immediate reduction in rates of abuse. At the end of the first year, 254 men have passed through the programme. Twelve have subsequently come to the attention of the police again, but it is too soon for the long term effectiveness of the programme to be evaluated.

Programmes such as HAIPP block the direct expression of physical aggression, some men may substitute for it other forms of intimidation and control but the women survivors are also learning that they do not have to put up with this. If they choose to stay in the relationship, they are supported in that choice and learn strategies to deal more equally with their dominating partners. The majority of the women feel safer as a result of their partner having completed the programme and feel that the men are more aware of the likely consequences of further violence (281). McMaster has produced a practical guide for men making changes which outlines a seven step process in detail and also contains a contact list of helpful resource groups (272).

There are several parallel developments for Maori men such as the fourteen groups of the Runanga Tane o Aotearoa (282). But there is a highly significant cultural difference. The whole programme of intervention and reform is directed by the iwi. These, then, are not simple men's groups in the sense of men dealing with angry violent men or with their own change. The community develops the action plans to stop the violence and takes into account all the factors which relate to the particular partnership or association. For example, within the mores of gangs, an incident of domestic violence is confronted by the whole gang community. In the process, a male chauvinist definition of being 'staunch' (loyal to one's mates before all else) is redefined so that the domestic incident is a violation against a group code (278). The motivation to change is, therefore, the shame of bringing dishonour to the group as well as a redefinition of the criteria of male strength, integrity and honour.

While groups that assist men to change their behaviour are on the increase, we should keep in mind that there are still all those other men's groups which are reinforcing the role supports for men to act violently. The bridging or outreach is just beginning. Men can change. Men are changing. There is now available good outcome information on the Kia Marama programme for sex offenders at Rolleston Prison where over a three year period only three cases of reoffending have occurred (269). The Kia Marama programme is not available, however, for all sex offenders. Such intensive programmes are too costly to waste on the unsuitable or the unwilling but they show that intensive therapy, applied to a selected population, is worth the cost. The programme is to be duplicated in the Auckland area.

Prison reform is gradually bringing about a revolution in institutional culture. For example, Unit Four at Paremoremo has adopted a new code where non-violence is developed, sustained and supported by the inmates themselves. New experiments in contract release of prisoners to community agencies, private enterprise prisons and residential parole to habilitation centres or to home detention could change the face of prison from its previous grim, grey shuffle of hopeless inmates to learning centres for the reformulation of life styles.

The justice system continues to suffer serious breakdown in the administration of non-molestation and domestic protection orders as shown in a recent report (263). This report includes 121 recommendations to improve the workings of the police, the family courts, and their counselling and the court system generally. The Department of Justice has indicated a readiness to act on almost all of these.

Even before the political decision was made to outlaw corporal punishment in schools much has been done through inservice professional education and support to develop alternate methods of discipline. A dramatic and successful programme called Cool

Schools operates in at least fourteen locations (277). Cool Schools
began because a class of children in 1984 asked their teacher,
Yvonne Duncan, if something could be done to resolve disputes
over marbles in the playground (267). World wars have begun over
disputes not much larger than these!

Cool Schools has a six step process which trains children to
become mediators in peer conflicts in classroom and playground.
The programme has been evaluated, has a detailed instruction kit
and runs demonstration workshops throughout the country. It
works.

There is still no definitive study on the relationship between
violent behaviour and traffic accidents and death. Recent information has revealed the rather staggering fact that forty-four percent
of drivers causing fatal accidents, have, on average, ten criminal convictions each (261). We strongly suspect that many of these will
relate to violent offending. Aggressive driving, risk-taking, bravado,
by young males or whoever, drunk or sober, needs to be understood,
countered, reduced. A man might just listen if his partner says,
'Dear, you are too drunk, I'll drive. Give me the keys.' But what are
the likely consequences if he or she were to say,' You are too angry,
let me drive.'

Legislative change is planned to restrict access to pornography
and semi-automatic weapons. The spotlight is turning strongly upon
the range of pornographic video material now freely available,
particularly where it depicts sex with, or between, children but even
as this occurs the entertainment industry is seeking new ways to
pander to the lust for violence as in the current, and we hope
temporary, craze for prize-fighting in pubs.

The new gun laws provide for separate and more expensive categories of licences for semi-automatic weapons and the relicensing
of all current licence holders. The police will have the power to con-
fiscate weapons found when they attend incidents of domestic
violence. But semi-automatic weapons can easily be modified to
avoid the increased licence fee and the gun lobby warns of the likelihood of widespread non-compliance with the new law.

The changes to gun laws are clearly inadequate since they do
nothing to reduce the availability of weapons but they were all the
politicians could achieve in a country where gun use is so deeply
entrenched in male tradition.

There is a growing groundswell against violent sports generally.
The probing eye of the television camera and the penchant for the
media to focus repetitively on illicit and violent acts has produced a
public reaction of revulsion. In desperation, rugby union administrators have modified the rules in an endeavour to reduce illicit
violence and to open up the game to make it faster. By these means

they hope to compete successfully with Rugby League for audience numbers (as well as to reduce injuries). But they have not changed the motivation of players and we repeat our conviction that rugby, union or league, is basically and intrinsically violent. We welcome the news that touch rugby is the most rapidly growing sport in the country. It is a fast non-contact game, played by men and women together. It is fun to play and entertaining to watch. Perhaps one day, in the not too distant future, rugby will only be played by consenting adults in private, and by players prepared to pay for their own injuries.

Two cities in New Zealand, that we know of, have attempted a coordinated approach to the reduction of violence. The Napier programme has been operating for at least five years but has not, however, affected the crime rate (274). Its continuance shows the tenacity with which a New Zealand community can hold on to a community development objective. It has achieved a measure of networking between discrete agencies and programmes which are directed at improving the quality of life, particularly for the disadvantaged. But in terms of making Napier free of violence, the programme lacks specific goals, a means of establishing priorities and is without evaluation except that required for the ongoing funding of the separate programmes.

More recently, community groups in Nelson joined together over one month to promote action for a non-violent community. Over thirty community groups focused their programme towards this goal and by the end of the month, Nelson, without doubt, dramatically raised public awareness and began to think and act programmatically, particularly in the area of non-violent child rearing and the alleviation of parental stress (271).

We do not doubt that there are many New Zealand communities which could act in similar ways, invite high profile speakers, make use of the media, improve networking and gain commitment from local authorities to sustain and support the programme. Perhaps from such grass roots activities a national wave of action might arise.

The first task of any change programme is to develop specific goals and relate them to the job descriptions and personal performance criteria of those who work to achieve these goals. Government policy now requires public agencies to perform in this way.

The New Zealand police both in their training modules and in their general policy statements are making considerable progress along these lines (266). In answer to the basic question, how can we reduce violent crime, they have isolated fifteen themes, each of which will require action well beyond that of traditional policing roles. For example, they emphasise that since violence is learnt, it can be unlearnt and that such learning involves what they call 'the bite of conscience'. Their strategic plan emphasises the importance of inter-agency cooperation.

In terms of their objectives, they have developed working objectives around such areas as drug control, child protection, domestic violence, target age groups, assistance for victims and witnesses, and concentration on at-risk youth. Their overall goal is focused on achieving public intolerance of violent crime by 1995 and significant reduction in its incidence by 1997.

This strategic plan has moved a long way from the traditional policing functions of the past.

Let us turn to the question of programming for change. In the last chapter we outlined sectors, targets and means for achieving change. We should now take the next step and ask how might a society like ours construct and implement such a programme. The sporadic and scattered nature of the progress which has been made over the last five years clearly indicates a serious lack: there is no clear and unitary ministerial responsibility for the reduction of violence. The Ministers of Justice and Police attend to crime, but that is too narrow a focus. The Ministries of Justice, Social Welfare and Police attend to the victims of crime, after the event. Various ministries have responsibilities to fund agencies such as women's refuges, Plunket, Parentline, rape crisis centres, men's groups, all of whom are seriously underfunded and overburdened. It is clearly not enough to merely have a vague and anonymous officials' committee to which politicians may point, but which never seems to report. The matter is simply too grave to be left at that level and to be subject to the whims of political sport, media beat-up or the sensation of the day or the week.

We would transcend the current responsibilities of both the bureaucracy and the politicians and place authority firmly in the hands of a Commissioner for the Reduction of Violence (279). This person would be charged with the task of negotiating bi-partisan policy, articulating the programme and monitoring performance. Such a commissioner would report directly to parliament and would have powers to initiate policy. The monitoring would be against explicit criteria derived from the framework of goals, targets and strategies. Such a model has already been developed in the ten health goals issued by the Department of Health in 1990 and now the responsibility of the Public Health Commission.

Our personal selection of such goals would include:
*Encourage non-violent child rearing practices*
*Discourage violent sports*
*Reduce domestic violence*
*Eliminate child and sexual abuse*
*Reduce entertainment violence*

*Control gun possession and limit use*
*Promote prison reform*
*Outlaw pornography*
*Reduce male violence*
*Teach conflict resolution*
*Redirect defence to peaceful purposes*
*Develop community networks.*

But it would be the first task of the Commissioner to consult with the community, all the way from politicians to the public, to achieve a limited set of realisable goals which could then be transformed into specific targets for which strategies could be developed. This is essentially a programming task. It would be the job of the Commissioner to say, if you wish to achieve this goal, then here are the specific targets at which you should aim. Here also are the strategies to achieve your objective.

Furthermore, the Commissioner would monitor progress on a yearly basis and produce a social balance sheet from which reassessment could be made for the coming year. We are quite sure that with such a programme we would not need to wait for a long time to see progress in these matters. Nor do we need any more background or single issue research before action is taken. What is needed is action research, evaluating interventions as has been done with Kia Marama or HAIPP.

Constructing a less violent society cannot be done without cost. The financial costs of change may well balance out. It has been estimated that the cost of male criminal violence alone totals over a billion dollars and when we add to this the costs of violent sport, aggressive driving, the hidden costs of domestic violence, the costs of counselling for sexual abuse victims we can probably double this figure. The country spends this in hope with no obvious reduction in violence.

To achieve a less violent society, money would have to be spent on the Commission and its activities and the funding of various programmes under its direction. The costs of a national programme of this kind may seem hard to meet, but the immediate and future savings will progressively reduce the financial load we are now forced to carry.

But we must approach the question of cost in another way. We are all survivors in a violent society. Just as the victim of a heart attack must give up certain pleasures and indulgences to return to health, so there are costs which must be paid, both socially and personally, to achieve the goal of becoming less violent. In men's workshops individuals may be asked to construct their personal list of the specific behaviours which they are prepared to give up. Those working with abusive parents will usually prohibit any physical punishment in order to break people out of the complacent and dangerous use of physical punishment.

Because we value freedom and liberty for all, we provide opportunities for the violent to find victims. In such matters as pornographic videos, gun control, war games in video parlours, and in many other areas we have mentioned in this book we are asking that the majority curtail some freedoms that they currently enjoy in order to protect us all from the minority who abuse such freedoms. It is unrealistic and unfair to expect some single agency, the police, for example, to deal with the consequences of the double message which society gives when it abhors, on the one hand, yet permits, on the other.

In the last analysis, this is a personal question which we address to each of our readers, as we daily address it to ourselves. What personal freedoms are you prepared to give up in order to enhance the peacefulness of our society? Are you prepared to give up watching, playing and supporting violent sports? Are you prepared to gently intervene when a parent hits a child in the street or in the supermarket? Will you forgo your weekly ration of hard action videos and television programmes?

If violence could simply be reduced by spending money, we would long since have achieved a peaceable society. But what we now see is that there is resistance to change because of the personal, social and cultural costs, the habits which must be relinquished, changes which can be specified but not quantified; these are the real costs which must be paid. Change begins at home.

# References

1. Accident Compensation Corporation (1988) *Annual Report*
2. Adler, A. (1928) *Understanding Human Nature* London: Allen & Unwin
3. Adorno, T.W., Frenkel-Brunswik, E., Levinson, D., and Sanford, N. (1950) *The Authoritarian Personality* New York: Harper
4. Albin, R.S. (1977) 'Psychological Studies of Rape' *Signs*, 3, 2, pp. 423–435.
5. Allport, G.W. (1937) *Personality: A Psychological Interpretation* New York: Holt
6. Anderson, M. (1963) *A River Rules My Life* Wellington: A.H. & A.W. Reed
7. Archer, D. and Gartner, R. (1984) *Violence and Crime in Cross-national Perspective* New Haven: Yale University Press
8. Ardrey, R. (1961) *African Genesis* London: Collins
9. Asher, B. (1988) *Reoffending and Parole* Wellington: Policy and Research Division, Department of Justice
10. Atmore, C. (1984) 'Pornography' *Broadsheet* 164, pp. 16–19, December
11. Atyeo, D. (1979) *Blood and Guts: Violence in Sports* New York: Paddington Press
12. Bailey, J. and Carpinter, Adele (in press) *Drink Driving in New Zealand* Wellington: D.S.I.R.
13. Bandura, A. (1973) *Aggression: a Social-learning Analysis* Engelwood Cliffs, New Jersey: Prentice-Hall
14. Barber, D. (1990) 'An Indecent Obsession' *Listener & T.V. Times* pp. 26–27, March 5
15. Barker, Lady M.A. (1953) *Station Life in New Zealand* Christchurch: Whitcombe and Tombs (first published 1873)

16. Bart, P.B., Freeman, L. and Kimball, P. (1985) 'The Different Worlds of Women and Men: Attitudes towards Pornography and Responses to Not a Love Story — A film about Pornography' *Women's Studies International Forum* 8, 4, pp. 307–322
17. Bateson, G. (1958) *Naven* Stanford: Stanford University Press
18. Bateson, G. (1979) *Mind and Nature: a Necessary Unity* New York: Dutton
19. Baxter, A. (1968) *We Will Not Cease* Christchurch: Caxton (first published 1939)
20. Beaglehole, A. (1988) *A Small Price to Pay: Refugees from Hitler in New Zealand, 1936–46* Wellington: Allen & Unwin/PNP
21. Belich, J. (1986) *The New Zealand Wars, and the Victorian Interpretation of Racial Conflict* Auckland: Auckland University Press
22. Belich, J. (1989) *I Shall Not Die: Titokowaru's War New Zealand, 1868–9* Wellington: Allen & Unwin/Port Nicholson Press
23. Belson, W.A. (1978) *Television Violence and the Adolescent Boy* Farnborough: Saxon House
24. Benedict, R. (1935) *Patterns of Culture* London: Routledge & Kegan Paul
25. Berkowitz, L. and Le Page, A. (1967) 'Weapons as Aggression – Eliciting Stimuli' *Journal of Personality and Social Psychology* pp. 202–207
26. Berkowitz, L. (1981) 'How Guns Control Us' *Psychology Today* June
27. Bernard, J. (1974) *The Future of Motherhood* New York: Dial Press
28. Borofsky, R. (1987) *Making History: Pukapuka and Anthropological Constructions of Knowledge* New York: Cambridge University Press
29. Bradbury, J. (1985) *Violent Offending and Drinking Patterns* Wellington: Institute of Criminology, Victoria University
30. Brownmiller, S. (1975) *Against Our Will: Men, Women, and Rape* New York: Simon & Schuster
31. Bunkle, P. (1988) *Second Opinion* Auckland: Oxford University Press
32. Bunkle, P. and Coney, S. (1987) 'An Unfortunate Experiment at National Women's Hospital' *Metro* June, pp. 46–65
33. Burt, M.R. (1980) 'Cultural Myths and Support for Rape' *Journal of Personality and Social Psychology* 38, pp. 217–230
34. Casswell, S. (1980) *Drinking by New Zealanders: Results of a National Survey of New Zealanders Aged 14–65* Auckland: Alcoholic Liquor Advisory Council, Alcohol Research Unit
35. Chester, R.H. and McMillian, N.A.C. (1981) *The Encyclopedia of New Zealand Rugby* Auckland: Moa Publications and Dominion Breweries
36. Church, J. (1978) *How to Get Out of Your Marriage Alive* Christchurch: John Church
37. Church, J. (1986) *Violence Against Wives: Its Causes and Effects* Christchurch: John Church
38. Cleave, P. (1989) *The Sovereignty Game* Wellington: Institute of Policy Studies/Victoria University Press
39. Coddington, C. and Marrieskind, L. (1982) 'Rape: an Analysis of Calls to the Hamilton Rape Crisis Centre' in Jane Ritchie (ed.)

*Psychology of Women, Research Record IV* Hamilton: University of Waikato

40. Coddington, C. (1984) 'Teachers Attitudes Towards Corporal Punishment: a Comparison of "User" and "Non-user" Schools' Unpublished Paper, Department of Psychology, University of Waikato

41. Committee on Health and Social Education (1977) *Growing, Sharing, Learning* (The Johnson Report) Wellington: Department of Education

42. Coney, S. (1988) *An Unfortunate Experiment* Auckland: Penguin

43. Conrad, P. (1988) 'Learning to Doctor – Reflections on Recent Accounts of the Medical School Years' *Journal of Health and Social Behaviour* 29, 4, pp. 323-332

44. Cupit, C.G. (1985) *Kids and the Scary World of Video* South Australian Council for Children's Films and Television Inc

45. Davis, A.F. (1973) *American Heroine: The Life and Legend of Jane Addams* New York: Oxford University Press

46. Deane, H. (1988) *The Social Effects of Imprisonment on Male Prisoners and their Families* Wellington: Institute of Criminology, Victoria University

47. De Mause, L. (1974) *The History of Childhood* New York: Psychohistory Press

48. Department of Justice (1983) *Rape Study* (2 vols) Wellington: Department of Justice

49. Department of Justice (1986) *Submission to the Committee of Inquiry into Violence* Wellington: Department of Justice

50. Department of Maori Affairs (1988) *Tirohanga Rangapu* Wellington: Department of Maori Affairs

51. Department of Maori Affairs (1988) *Urupare Rangapu* Wellington: Department of Maori Affairs

52. Donnelly, F. (1978) *Big Boys Don't Cry* Auckland: Cassell

53. Donnelly, F. (1988) *The World Upside Down* Auckland: Penguin

54. Donnerstein, E. and Berkowitz. U. (1981) 'Victim Reactions in Aggressive Erotic Films as a Factor in Violence Against Women' *Journal of Personality and Social Psychology* 41, 4, pp. 710–724

55. Dyall, J.R. and Mako, C. (1985) *Negative Funding and Inequity* Wellington: Maori Economic Development Commission

56. Elsmore, B. (1989) *Mana From Heaven: A Century of Maori Prophets in New Zealand* Tauranga: Moana Press

57. Enock, Y. (1989) 'Change of Values During Socialization for a Profession' *Human Relations* 42, 3, pp. 219–239

58. Eron, L.D. (1982) 'Parent–Child Interaction, Television Violence, and Aggression in Children' *American Psychologist* 37, pp. 197–211

59. Fergusson, D.M., Fleming, J., and O'Neill, D.P. (1972) *Child Abuse in New Zealand* Wellington: Government Print

60. Fergusson, D.M., Horward, L.J., Kershaw, K.L. and Shannon, F.T. (1986) 'Factors Associated with Reports of Wife Assault in New Zealand' *Journal of Marriage and the Family*, 48, 2, pp. 407–412

61.  Finkelhor, D. (1978) *Sexually Victimized Children* New York: Free Press
62.  Finkelhor, D. and Yllo, K. (1983) 'Rape in Marriage: A Sociological View', in D. Finkelhor, R.J. Gelles, G.T. Hotaling, M.A. Straus (eds) *The Dark Side of Families: Current Family Violence Research* Beverley Hills: Sage
63.  Flynn, E. (1988) 'Child Abuse: The Facts' *NZ Listener* August 13, pp. 16–18
64.  Ford, C. and Beach, F.A. (1951) *Patterns of Sexual Behaviour* New York: Paul Moeber
65.  Ford, G.W. (1987) *Research Project on Domestic Disputes: Final Report* Wellington: N.Z. Police National Headquarters
66.  Fougere, G. (1989) 'Sport, Culture and Identity: The Case of Rugby Football' in D. Novitz and B. Willmott (eds) *Culture and Identity in New Zealand* Wellington: Government Print
67.  Frank, L.K. (1948) *Society and the Patient* New Brunswick: Rutgers University Press
68.  Freud, S. (1975) *The Psychopathology of Everyday Life* Harmondsworth, Middlesex: Penguin (first published 1901)
69.  Freud, S. (1920) *A General Introduction to Psychoanalysis* New York: Boni & Liveright
70.  Freud, S. (1930) *Civilization and its Discontents* London: Hogarth Press
71.  Fromm, E. (1942) *The Fear of Freedom* London: Routledge & Kegan Paul
72.  Fromm, E. (1974) *The Anatomy of Human Destructiveness* London: Jonathan Cape
73.  Geddis, D.C. (1980) *Child Abuse, Report of a National Symposium* Dunedin: National Children's Health Foundation
74.  Geen. R.G., Stonner, D. and Shope, G.L. (1975) 'The Facilitation of Aggression by Aggression: Evidence Against the Catharsis Hypothesis' *Journal of Personality and Social Psychology* 31, pp. 721–726
75.  Geen, R.G. & O'Neal, E. (eds) (1976) *Perspectives on Aggression* New York: Academic Press
76.  Gelles, R.J. (1974) *The Violent Home: A Study of Physical Aggression Between Husbands and Wives* Beverley Hills: Sage Publications
77.  Gelles, R.J. (1979) *Family Violence* Beverley Hills: Sage Publications
78.  Giles-Sims, J. (1979) *Stability and Change in Patterns of Wife-beating: a Systems Theory Approach* Ph.D. dissertation. University of New Hampshire
79.  Goldman, I. (1970) *Ancient Polynesian Society* Chicago: Chicago University Press
80.  Goldstein, A.P. (1983) *Prevention and Control of Aggression* New York: Permagon Press
81.  Goldstein, J. (1983) *Sports Violence* New York: Springer-Velag
82.  Goldstein, J.H. and Arms, R.L. (1971). 'Effects of Observing Athletic Contests on Hostility' *Sociometry* 34(1), pp. 83–90.
83.  Goode, W.J. (1971) 'Force and Violence in the Family' *Journal of Marriage and the Family* 33(4) pp. 624–636

84. Goodyear-Smith, F.A. (1989) 'Medical Evaluation of Sexual Assault Findings in the Auckland Region' *New Zealand Medical Journal* 102, pp. 493–495
85. Grant, D. (1986) *Out in the Cold* Auckland: Methuen
86. Graves, T.D. and N.B. (1979) *Drinking and Violence in a Multi-cultural Society* Research Report No. 21 Henderson, Auckland: South Pacific Research Institute
87. Gray, A. (1989) *Family Violence: A Background Paper* Wellington: Gray Matter Research Ltd
88. Grimshaw, P. (1972) *Women's Suffrage in New Zealand* Auckland: Auckland University Press
89. Haines, H. (1983) *Violence on Television: A Report on the Mental Health Foundation's Media Watch Survey* Auckland: Mental Health Foundation of New Zealand
90. Haines, H. (1986) *Report on Video Survey* Auckland: Mental Health Foundation
91. Haines, H. and Abbot, M. (eds.) (1983) *Rape in New Zealand* Auckland: Mental Health Foundation
92. Hamilton, I. (1984) *Till Human Voices Wake Us* Auckland: Auckland University Press (first published 1953)
93. Hay, J. (1986) *Teachers and Child Abuse Prevention: a Study of Teachers' Knowledge, Attitudes and Behaviour Before and After Training Programmes* Masters Thesis. Hamilton: University of Waikato
94. Helmich, E. (1985) *The Effectiveness of Preschool for Children from Low-Income Families: A Review of the Literature* Springfield: Illinois State Board of Education
95. Hite, S. (1981) *The Hite Report on Male Sexuality* New York: Knopf
96. Hodge, K. (1988) *Character Building in Sport: Fact or Fiction?* Paper presented at the New Zealand Psychology Society Conference, University of Waikato
97. Horney, K. (1937) *The Neurotic Personality of Our Time* New York: Norton
98. Horney, K. (1942) *Self-analysis* New York: Norton
99. Howard, A., and Borofsky, R. (1989) *Developments in Polynesian Ethnology* Honolulu: University of Hawaii Press
100. Huesmann, L.R., Eron, L.D., Lefkowitz, M.M. and Walder, L.O. (1984) 'Stability of Aggression Over Time and Generations' *Developmental Psychology* 20, pp. 1120–1134
101. Hull, C. (1966) *Principles of Behaviour: an Introduction to Behaviour Theory* New York: Appleton – Century – Crofts
102. Hunn, J.K. (1961) *Report on Department of Maori Affairs* Wellington: Government Print
103. Jackson, M. (1988) *The Maori and the Criminal Justice System: a New Perspective – He Whaipaanga Hou* Wellington: Policy and Research Division, Dept of Justice
104. James, W. (1911) 'The Moral Equivalent of War' in H. James (ed.) *Memories and Studies* New York: Holt
105. Kaufman, J. and Zigler, E. (1987) 'Do Abused Children Become Abusive Parents?' *American Journal of Orthopsychiatry* 57, pp. 186–192

106. Kawharu, I.H. (ed.) (1989) *Waitangi: Maori and Pakeha Perspectives of the Treaty of Waitangi* Auckland: Oxford University Press

107. Kelsey, J. (1990) *A Question of Honour? Labour and the Treaty 1984–1989* Wellington: Allen and Unwin/PNP

108. Kelsey, J. and Young, W. (1982) *The Gangs: Moral Panic as Social Control* Wellington: Institute of Criminology, Victoria University

109. Kempe, C., Silverman, F., Steele, B., Droegmueller, W. and Silver, H. (1962) 'The Battered Child Syndrome' *Journal of the American Medical Association* 181, pp. 17–24

110. Kempe, C.H. (1978) 'Recent Developments in the Field of Child Abuse' *Child Abuse and Neglect* 2(4), pp. 261–267

111. King, M. (1977) *Te Puea: a Biography* Auckland: Hodder & Stoughton

112. King, M. (1989) *Moriori: A People Rediscovered* Auckland: Viking

113. Kinsey, A.S., Pomeroy, W.E., and Martin C.E. (1948) *Sexual Behavior in the Human Male* Philadelphia: Saunders

114. Kinsey, A.S. (1953) *Sexual Behavior in the Human Female* Philadelphia: Saunders

115. Kissing, B. & Begleiter, H. (1976) *Social Aspects of Alcoholism* New York: Plenum Press

116. Koop, E.E. (1987) 'Report of the Surgeon General's Workshop on Pornography and Public Health' *American Psychologist* 42, 10, pp. 944–945

117. Kubler-Ross, E. (1969) *On Death and Dying* New York: McMillan

118. Kubler-Ross, E. (1972) *Living with Death and Dying* London: Souvenir Press

119. Kurian, G.T. (1979) *Book of World Rankings* New York: Facts on File

120. Kutash, I.L., Kutash, S.B. and Schlesinger, L.B. (1978) *Violence: Perspectives on Murder and Aggression* San Francisco: Jossey-Bass

121. Leakey, R.E. (1977) *Origins: What New Discoveries Reveal About the Emergence of Our Species and its Possible Future* London: MacDonald & Jane's

122. Leakey, R.E. (1981) *The Making of Mankind* London: M. Joseph

123. Lederer, L. (ed.) (1980) *Take Back the Night* New York: W. Morrow

124. Lederer, L. (1980) 'Playboy Isn't Playing: An Interview With Judith Bat-Ada' in L. Lederer (ed.) *Take Back the Night* New York: W. Morrow

125. Levy, R. (1969) 'On Getting Angry in the Society Islands' in W. Caudill and T. Lin (eds.) *Mental Health Research in Asia and the Pacific* Honolulu: East-West Centre Press

126. Lewin, K. (1948) *Resolving Social Conflicts, Selected Papers on Group Dynamics* New York: Harper

127. Lewis, Paul (1989) 'The Arming of New Zealand' *Sunday Magazine* 29 October, pp. 28–38

128. Liebert, R.M., Neale, J.M. and Davidson, E.S. (1973) *The Early Window: Effects of Television on Children and Youth* New York: Pergamon

129. Lorenz, K.Z. (1966) *On Aggression* London: Methuen
130. McAndrew, C., and Edgerton, R.B. (1970) *Drunken Comportment: A Social Explanation* London: Nelson
131. McGee, G. (1981) *Foreskin's Lament* Wellington: Victoria University Press
132. Maclean, C. and Phillips, J. (1990) *The Sorrow and the Pride: New Zealand War Memorials* Wellington: Government Print
133. McLuhan, M. (1967) *The Medium is the Message* New York: Basic Books
134. McMaster, K. and Swain, P. (1989) *A Private Affair? Stopping Men's Violence to Women* Wellington: Government Print
135. Maccoby, E.E. and Jacklin, C.N. (1974) *The Psychology of Sex Differences* Stanford: Stanford University Press
136. Mahon, P. (1984) Report of Committee of Inquiry into the Riot at Auckland on 7th December, 1984
137. Malamuth, N.M., Haber, S., and Feshback, S. (1980) 'Testing Hypotheses Regarding Rape: Exposure to Sexual Violence, Sex Differences, and the 'Normality' of Rapists' *Journal of Research in Personality* 38(3), pp. 399–408
138. Marcus, G. (1989) 'Chieftainship' in A. Howard & R. Borofsky (eds.) *Developments in Polynesian Ethnology* Honolulu: University of Hawaii Press
139. Marlatt, G.A. & Rohsenow, D. (1981) 'The Think-drink Effect' *Psychology Today* December
140. Marsh, P. (1978) *Aggro: The Illusion of Violence* London: Dent
141. Masters, W.H. and Johnson, V.E. (1966) *Human Sexual Response* Boston: Little, Brown
142. Mead, M. (1935) *Sex and Temperament in Three Primitive Societies* New York: W. Morrow
143. Mental Health Foundation (1982) Papers presented at the Rape Symposium at Wellington
144. Mental Health Foundation (1984) *The Influence of the Media on the Behaviour of Young People* Auckland: Mental Health Foundation
145. Mental Health Foundation (1986) *The Prevention of Violence: Submission to the Ministerial Committee of Inquiry into Violence* Auckland: Mental Health Foundation
146. Miller, N. (1941) 'The Frustration Aggression Hypothesis' *Psychological Review* 48, pp. 337–342
147. Miller, N.E. and Dolland, J. (1941) *Social Learning and Imitation* New Haven: Yale University Press
148. Ministerial Advisory Committee on a Maori Perspective for the Department of Social Welfare (1986) *Puao-te-atatu (Daybreak)* Wellington: Department of Social Welfare
149. Ministerial Committee of Inquiry into Pornography (1989) Wellington
150. Ministerial Committee of Inquiry Into Violence (1987) *Report of Ministerial Committee of Inquiry Into Violence.* (The Roper Report) Wellington: Department of Justice

151. Ministerial Committee of Inquiry Into the Prison Systems (1989) *Prison Review: Te Ara-hou – The New Way* Wellington: Crown

152. Ministry of Transport (1988) *Road Accidents in New Zealand 1980–1987* Wellington: Ministry of Transport

153. Ministry of Transport (1989) *Road Transport: A Future Strategy* Wellington: Ministry of Transport

154. Monaghan, S. et al. (1986) Prenatal Screening for Risk of Major Parenting Problems: Further Results from the Queen Mary Hospital Child Care Unit *Child Abuse and Neglect* 10, pp. 369–375

155. Money, J. (1975) *Sexual Signatures: On Being a Man or a Woman* Boston: Little, Brown

156. Montagu, M.F.A. (ed) (1968) *Man and Aggression* New York: Oxford University Press

157. Morgan, R. (1982) *The Anatomy of Freedom* New York: Anchor Press/Doubleday

158. Morris, D. (1967) *The Naked Ape: a Zoologist's Study of the Human Animal* London: Cape

159. Mulgan, J. (1930) *Man Alone* Hamilton: Selwyn and Blount

160. Mulgan, R. (1979) *Maori, Pakeha and Democracy* Auckland: Oxford University Press

161. Mullen, P., Romans-Clarkson, S., Herbison, P. & Walton, W. (1988) Impact of Sexual and Physical Abuse on Women's Mental Health *The Lancet* April 16

162. National Advisory Committee on the Prevention of Child Abuse (1986) *Guidelines for the Investigation of Management and Child Abuse* Wellington: National Advisory Committee on Prevention of Child Abuse

163. National Collective of Independent Women's Refuges Inc (1983) *A Socio-economic Assessment of New Zealand Women's Refuges* Blenheim: National Collective of Independent Women's Refuges Inc

164. National Collective of Independent Women's Refuges Inc. (1989) *Home is Where the Hurt is* Pamphlet

165. New Zealand Committee on Gangs (1981) *The Comber Report on Gangs* Wellington: Government Print

166. Novaco, R.W. (1975) *Anger Control* Lexington Books

167. Oliver, D. (1974) *Ancient Tahitian Society* Honolulu: University of Hawaii Press

168. Orange, C. (1987) *The Treaty of Waitangi* Wellington: Allen & Unwin/PNP

169. Orange, C. (1989) *The Story of a Treaty* Wellington: Allen & Unwin/PNP

170. Pagelow, M.D. (1980) *Does the Law Help Battered Wives? Some Research Notes* Madison, Wisconsin: Law and Society Association

171. Parham, W.T. (1969) *Von Tempsky – Adventurer* London: Hodder and Stoughton

172. Penal Policy Review Committee (1981) *Report of the Penal Policy Review Committee* Wellington: Department of Justice

173. Phillips, J. (1984) 'Rugby, War and the Mythology of the New Zealand Male' *New Zealand Journal of History* 18, 2, pp. 83–103

174. Phillips, J. (1987) *A Man's Country? The Image of the Pakeha Male: A History* Auckland: Penguin

175. Phillips, J. (1989) 'War and National Identity' in D. Novitz and B. Willmot (eds) *Culture and Identity in New Zealand* Wellington: Government Print
176. Porter, F. (1989) *Born to New Zealand, A Biography of Jane Maria Atkinson* Wellington: Allen & Unwin/PNP
177. Pow, G. (1986) *The Psychological Consequences of Sexual Assault: a Literature Review* Wellington: Accident Compensation Corporation
178. Pugsley, C. (1984) *Gallipoli: The New Zealand Story* Auckland: Hodder and Stoughton
179. Radice, L. (1984) *Beatrice and Stanley Webb: Fabian Socialists* London: McMillan
180. Rayner, T., Chetwynd, J. & Alexander, T. (1984) *Costs of Alcohol Abuse in New Zealand* Alcoholic Liquor Advisory Council of NZ
181. Riseborough H. (1989) *Days of Darkness* Wellington: Allen & Unwin/PNP
182. Ritchie, James E. (1963) *The Making of a Maori* Wellington: A.H. & A.W. Reed
183. Ritchie, James (1988) *Sacred Chiefs and Secular Gods: The Polynesian World View* Hamilton: Centre for Maori Studies and Research, University of Waikato
184. Ritchie, Jane (1957) *Childhood in Rakau; the First Five Years of Life* Masters Thesis, Department of Psychology, Victoria University
185. Ritchie, Jane (1979) 'Child Rearing Patterns: Further Studies' *Psychology Research Series* No. 11 Hamilton: University of Waikato
186. Ritchie, Jane (1980) *Speak Roughly to Your Little Boy and Beat Him When He Sneezes* Paper Presented at Women's Studies Association Conference, Auckland
187. Ritchie, Jane (1981) *Boys will be Boys* Paper presented at Women's Studies Association Conference, Wellington
188. Ritchie, Jane (1982) *Taught to the Tune of a Hickory Stick: Corporal Punishment and Attitudes to Violence in Secondary School Students* Paper Presented at Women's Studies Conference, Palmerston North
189. Ritchie, Jane (1986) 'Pornography and Sexual Violence Against Women' in D. Braun and J. Koirala (eds.) *Entertainment Violence and a Peaceful World,* Auckland: Mental Health Foundation of New Zealand
190. Ritchie, Jane (1988) 'Commerce or Con: Young People and Cigarette Advertising' *Community Health Studies* Vol. 12(1), pp. 9–15
191. Ritchie, Jane (1988) *Motherhood in the Eighties: Some Childrearing Comparisons* Paper presented to the New Zealand Psychological Society Conference, Hamilton
192. Ritchie, Jane and James (1970) *Child Rearing Patterns in New Zealand* Wellington: A.H. & A.W. Reed
193. Ritchie, Jane and James (1978) *Growing up in New Zealand* Sydney: Allen & Unwin
194. Ritchie, Jane and James (1979) *Growing up in Polynesia* Sydney: Allen & Unwin
195. Ritchie, Jane and James (1980) Unpublished Data: Parents' Attitudes to Physical Punishment

196. Ritchie, Jane and James (1981) Unpublished Data: Physical Punishment of Third and Fourth Form Students
197. Ritchie, Jane and James (1981) *Spare the Rod* Sydney: Allen & Unwin
198. Ritchie, Jane and James (1983) 'New Zealand Developmental and Social Antecedants and Concomitants of Aggression' in A.P. Goldstein and M.H. Segall (eds.) *Aggression in Global Perspective* New York: Pergamon Press
199. Ritchie, Jane and James (1984) *The Dangerous Age* Sydney: Allen & Unwin
200. Ritchie, Jane and James (1985) *E Tipu E Rea: Polynesian Socialisation and Psychological Development.* Hamilton: Centre for Maori Studies, University of Waikato.
201. Ritchie, Jane and James (1986) *Submission to Ministerial Committee of Inquiry into Violence* Hamilton: University of Waikato
202. Ritchie, Jane and James (1988) Unpublished Data: Attitudes to Violence
203. Ritchie, Jane and James (1988) 'Socialisation and Psychological Development' in A. Howard and R. Borofsky (eds) *Developments in Polynesian Ethnology* Honolulu: University of Hawaii Press
204. Ritchie, Jane, Paine, H. and Tourelle, L. (1980) 'Sex Differences in Physical Punishment: The Children's View' in Jane Ritchie (ed.) *Psychology of Women: Research Record III* Hamilton: University of Waikato
205. Rodin, J. Silberstein, L. and Striegel Moore, R. (1984) *Women and Weight: A Normative Discontent* Nebraska: Nebraska Symposium on Motivation
206. Romanos, J. (1989) 'State of the Sporting Nation' *NZ Listener* September 9, pp. 20–25
207. Rose, R.M., Gordon, R.P. and Bernstein, I.S. (1972) 'Plasma Testosterone Levels in the Male Rhesus: Influence of Sexual and Social Stimuli' *Science* 178, pp. 643–645
208. Royal Commission on Broadcasting and Related Telecommunications in New Zealand (1986) Broadcasting and Related Telecommunications in New Zealand, Auckland
209. Royal Commission on Social Policy (1988) *Towards a Fair and Just Society* Wellington: Government Print
210. Royal Commission on Social Policy (1988) *Report of the Royal Commission on Social Policy* Wellington: Government Print
211. Russell, D. (1980) 'Pornography and Violence: What Does the New Research Say?' in L. Lederer (ed) *Take Back the Night* New York: W. Morrow
212. Russell, D. (1980) *The Prevalence and Impact of Marital Rape in San Francisco* Paper presented at the annual meeting of the American Sociological Association, New York
213. Rutherford, J. (1961) *Sir George Grey* London: Cassell
214. Rutter, M. and Madge, N. (1976) *Cycles of Disadvantage: A Review of Research* London: Heinemann

215. Ryan, A. (1988) 'Policing Pornography. A Repressive Strategy' *Broadsheet* 158, pp. 38–41, May
216. Sabo, D. and Runfola, R. (1980) *Jock: Sport and Male Identity* Englewood Cliffs New Jersey: Prentice Hall
217. Sahlins, M. (1985) *Islands of History* Chicago: Chicago University Press
218. Sanday, P.R. (1981) 'The Socio-cultural Context of Rape: a Cross-cultural Study' *Journal of Social Issues* 37, 4, pp. 5–27
219. Saphira, M. (1981) *The Sexual Abuse of Children* Ponsonby: Papers Inc
220. Secker, E.W. (1887) *On the Ball: A Football Song* Dunedin: Charles Begg
221. Select Committee on Violent Offending (1979) *Report to the House of Representatives* Wellington: Government Print
222. Shadbolt, M. (1982) *Once on Chunuk Bair* Auckland: Hodder and Stoughton
223. Shadbolt, M. (1988) *Voices of Gallipoli* Auckland: Hodder and Stoughton
224. Shapcott, D. (1988) *The Face of the Rapist* Auckland: Penguin
225. Shore, B. (1989) 'Mana and Tapu' in A. Howard and R. Borofsky (eds.) *Developments in Polynesian Ethnology* Honolulu: University of Hawaii Press
226. Shuntich, R.J. and Taylor, S.P. (1972) 'The Effects of Alcohol on Human Physical Aggression' *Journal of Experimental Research in Personality* 6, pp. 34–38
227. Singer, J.L. and Singer, D.C. (1981) *Television, Imagination, and Aggression: a Study of Preschoolers* Hilldale, New Jersey: L. Erlbaum Associates
228. Singh, J. and Rosier, P. (1989) *No Body's Perfect* Auckland: New Women's Press
229. Spektor, P. (1980) Testimony Delivered to the Law Enforcement Subcommittee of the Minnesota House of Representatives, February 29th
230. Spoonley, Paul (1981) New Zealand First: The Extreme Right and Politics in New Zealand 1961–1981. Winter Lecture Series, University of Waikato
231. Stace, M. (1983) 'Rape Complaints and the Police' *Rape Study* Volume 2, Wellington: Department of Justice
232. Star, L. (1989) *Masculinity Rituals and Televised Rugby* Paper presented to Women's Studies Association Conference, Christchurch
233. Steele, B.F. and Pollick, C.B. (1974) 'A Psychiatric Study of Parents Who Abuse Infants and Small Children' in R.E. Helfer and C.H. Kempe (eds) *The Battered Child* pp 89–134, Chicago: Chicago University of Press
234. Steinem, G. (1980) 'Erotica and Pornography: a Clear and Present Difference', in L. Lederer (ed) *Take Back the Night* New York: W. Morrow

235. Steinmetz, S.K. and Straus M. (1974) *Violence in the Family* New York: Harper and Row

236. Stone, J.C., Barrington, R. and Bevan, C. (1983) 'The Victim Survey' *Rape Study* Volume 2, Wellington: Department of Justice

237. Stout Centre Fifth Annual Conference (1988) A War-like People? – War in New Zealand Experience (Unpublished papers)

238. Straus, M. and Gelles, R. (1986) 'Societal Change and Change in Family Violence from 1975 to 1985 As Revealed by Two National Surveys' *Journal of Marriage and the Family* 48, pp. 465–479

239. Straus, M., Gelles, R. and Steinmetz, S. (1980) *Behind Closed Doors: Violence in the American Family* New York: Anchor Books

240. Surgeon General's Scientific Advisory Committee on Television and Social Behaviour (1972) *Television and Growing Up: the Impact of Televised Violence* Washington: U.S. Government Print Office

241. Taskforce to Review Education Administration (1988) *Administrating for Excellence: Effective Administration in Education* (Picot Report) Wellington: Taskforce to Review Education Administration

242. Tauroa, H. (1989) *Healing the Breach* Auckland: Collins

243. Taylor, S.P. and Gammon, C. (1975) 'The Effects of Type and Dose of Alcohol on Human Aggression' *Journal of Experimental Research in Personality* 32, pp. 169–175

244. Taylor, S.P. and Leonard, K.E. (1983) 'Alcohol and Human Physical Aggression' in R. Green and E. Donnenstein (eds) *Aggression: Theoretical and Empirical Reviews* New York: Academic Press

245. Temm, P. (1990) *The Waitangi Tribunal: The Conscience of the Nation* Auckland: Random Century

246. Thomas, D.R. (1989) *Cultural Pluralism and Development: Applications in Education and Learning* Hamilton: University of Waikato

247. Tierney, K.J. and Corwin, D.L. (1983) 'Exploring Intrafamilial Child Sexual Abuse: A Systems Approach', in D. Finkelhor, R.J. Gelles, G.T. Hotaling, M.A. Straus (eds) *The Dark Side of Families* Beverley Hills: Sage

248. Toxic Substances Board (1989) *Health or Tobacco* Wellington: Department of Health

249. Tsoulis, A. (1986) 'Pornography and Censorship' *Broadsheet* pp. 35–37, August

250. Turner, C.W. and Goldsmith, D. (1976) 'Effects of Toy Guns and Airplanes on Children's Antisocial Free Play Behavior' *Journal of Experimental Child Psychology* 21, pp. 303–315

251. Turner, C.W., Layton, J.F. and Simons, L.S. (1975) 'Naturalistic Studies of Aggressive Behavior: Aggressive Stimuli, Victim Visibility and Horn Honking' *Journal of Social and Personality Psychology* 31, pp. 1098–1107

252. UNESCO (1950) *Tensions Affecting International Understanding: A Survey of Research* New York: Social Science Research Council

253. Van Dadelszen, J. (1987) *Sexual Abuse Study: An Examination of the*

*Histories of Sexual Abuse Among Girls Currently in the Care of the Department of Social Welfare* Wellington: Department of Social Welfare

254.  Warren, H., Griffiths, C. and Huygens, I. (1989) *Our Shout: Women and Alcohol* Auckland: Heinemann Reed

255.  Whiting, B. and Edwards, C.P. (1973) 'A Cross-Cultural Analysis of Sex Differences in the Behaviour of Children Aged Three Through Eleven' *Journal of Social Psychology* 91(2), pp. 171–188

256.  Wolfe, T. (1970) *Radical Chic and Mau-Mauing the Flak Catchers* New York: Farrer, Straus and Giroux

257.  Women Against Pornography (1988) *Summary of Wellington Women Against Pornography's Submission to the Committee of Inquiry into Pornography* Wellington: Women Against Pornography.

258.  Yensen, H., Hague, K. and McCreanan, T. (1989) *Honouring the Treaty: An Introduction for Pakeha to the Treaty of Waitangi* Auckland: Penguin Books

259.  Young, W. (1983) *Rape Study* Wellington: Department of Justice

260.  Zimring, F.E. (1985) 'American Violence and Public Policy' in L.A, Curtis (ed.) *American Violence and Public Policy* New Haven: Yale University Press

# Supplementary References

261. Bailey, J.P.M. (1993) *Criminal and Traffic Histories, Blood Alcohol and Accident Characteristics of Drivers in Fatal Road Accidents in New Zealand* Lower Hutt: Institute of Environmental Health and Forensic Sciences

262. Binstead, J. (1992) *The Men For Non-Violence (NZ) Network and Community Stopping Violence and Sex Offender Programmes* Auckland: Mental Health Foundation of New Zealand, and AIT: Prevention of Violence Conference Proceedings

263. Busch, R., Robertson, R. and Lapsley, H. (1992) *Domestic Violence and the Justice System. A Study of Breaches of Protection Orders* Wellington: Victims Task Force

264. Department of Health (1989) *New Zealand Health Goals and Targets* Wellington: Department of Health

265. Department of Justice (1992) *Implementation of the Recommendations of the Roper Report* Policy and Research Division. Wellington: Department of Justice

266. Doone, P.E.C. (1992) *Violent Crime – Achieving Public Intolerance by 1995 – Reducing the Incidence and Effects by 1997* Auckland: Mental Health Foundation of New Zealand, and AIT: Prevention of Violence Conference Proceedings

267. Duncan, Y. (1992) *Peace Education in Schools. Empowering Young People to Make a Choice* Auckland: Mental Health Foundation of New Zealand, and AIT: Prevention of Violence Conference Proceedings

268. EPOCH (1992) *Hitting People is Wrong and Children are People Too* London: Approach Ltd

269. Gherardi, P. (1992) *Police and Justice Issues* Auckland: Mental Health Foundation, and AIT: Prevention of Violence Conference Proceedings

270. Hassall, I. (1992) *Hitting Children* Children No. 7 Wellington: Commission for Children
271. McKeever, C. (1992) *Taking Action in Nelson: A Community Initiated Violence Prevention Project* Auckland: Mental Health Foundation, and AIT: Prevention of Violence Conference Proceedings
272 McMaster, K. (1992) *Feeling Angry: Playing Fair* Auckland: Reed
273. Mason, K. (1992) *Review of Children, Young Persons and Their Families Act* Wellington: Department of Social Welfare
274. Napier Pilot City Trust (1992) *Submission to National Seminar on the Prevention of Violence* Napier: Napier Pilot City Trust
275. Newbold, G. (1992) *Crime and Deviance* Auckland: Oxford University Press
276. Newell, P. (1989) *Children are People Too* London: Bedford Square Press
277. New Zealand Foundation for Peace Studies Inc. (1992) *The Cool Schools Peer Mediation Programme* Auckland: NZ Foundation for Peace Studies
278. Payne, B. (1991) *Staunch: Inside the Gangs* Reed: Auckland
279. Ritchie, J. (1991) *The Cultural Cost of Becoming Less Violent* Auckland: Mental Health Foundation of New Zealand, and AIT: Prevention of Violence Conference Proceedings
280. Robertson, N.R., Busch, R., Ave, K.T. and Balzer, R. (1991) *Hamilton Abuse Intervention Pilot Project: The First Three Months* University of Waikato: The HAIPP Monitoring Team
281. Robertson, N.R., Busch, R., Glover, M.P. and Furness, J.A. (1992) *Hamilton Abuse Intervention Project: The First Year* University of Waikato: The HAIPP Monitoring Team
282. Stirling, P. (1992) 'Stop the Bashings' *Listener and TV Times*, June 22
283. Walker, R. (1992) *Stopping Violence – Lessons Learnt at the Anger Management Coalface* Auckland: Mental Health Foundation of New Zealand, and AIT: Prevention of Violence Conference Proceedings

# Index